i AM
REMNANT

i AM REMNANT

PAT SCHATZLINE

PASSIO

I AM REMNANT by Pat Schatzline
Published by Passio
Charisma Media/Charisma House Book Group
600 Rinehart Road
Lake Mary, Florida 32746
www.charismahouse.com

Cover design by Justin Evans
Design Director: Bill Johnson

Visit the author's website at www.mercyseatministries.com.

Library of Congress Control Number: 2013920576
International Standard Book Number: 978-1-62136-576-1
E-book ISBN: 978-1-62136-577-8

First edition

14 15 16 17 18 — 9 8 7 6 5 4 3 2 1
Printed in the United States of America

I DEDICATE THIS BOOK to my best friend, my wife, and my sweetheart, Karen. You have always pushed me to dream big and trust God. Your purity and passion for Jesus have taught me what it means to be remnant. You have transformed thousands of lives with your messages of hope. You have taught our children that they are called to live lives that count for Jesus and to walk out their destiny with purpose. Thank you for believing that together we could change a generation. You are my hero! You are the wind beneath my wings.

CONTENTS

ACKNOWLEDGMENTS

THANK YOU TO my precious kids, Abby, Nate, and Adrienne, for standing with Dad as he takes these seasons to write. I am so proud of you. You are remnant!

Thank you to my parents, Bishop Patrick and Deb Schatzline, for teaching us the power of standing firm in purity, holiness, and truth.

Thank you to Pastor Larry Stockstill for writing *The Remnant: Restoring the Call to Personal Integrity*. That powerful book transformed my life and laid the groundwork for this one. Thank you, pastor, for speaking truth!

Thank you so much to my assistant, Jamie Kowalski, and Dr. Connie Lawrence not only for helping me organize this vision but also for helping to bring it to life on paper with your hard work. I couldn't have done it without you!

To the awesome team of leaders at Mercy Seat Ministries and the Forerunner School of Ministry: Thank you for your hard work and research for this project.

To Debbie Marrie, Adrienne Gaines, and the entire team at Charisma Media: You guys are awesome. Your hard work and vision inspire me.

Lastly, I have had the honor of meeting and walking with thousands of leaders all over the world who have made up their minds to be remnant. I want to say thank you to those leaders who are continuing to fight for the truth and are believing God can transform a generation. You are on the front lines every day, ministering life to the hurting and leading with distinction. God has His hands upon you! He has anointed you for such a time as this. Don't get weary in well doing. Your harvest will greet you in heaven. Let's turn the world upside down for Jesus! Acts 17:6!

FOREWORD

ARE YOU READY to make history? I mean really, really alter the annals of antiquity? Because it's on you! The novelist James Baldwin hit it on the head by saying, "People are trapped in history and history is trapped in them."[1]

I've recently come under the conviction that a generation of game-changers are going to emerge that history and heaven will never forget. This remnant will revolutionize their world, demonstrate the kingdom, and usher in the greatest harvest the world has ever seen. These forerunners have encoded in their DNA to break the curve set by the masses of people who have previously stepped up to the plate of human history. There are moments, and then there are *moments*.

There are defining moments in the history of every nation, and in each generation there are leaders who recognize and seize these opportunities. I believe America is on the threshold of a historic moment. I have been gripped by a promise of end-time awakeners who will be used of God in unprecedented fashion. They will bear the markings of a supernatural lifestyle and a people wholly given over to the Lord. They have reached a desperation point that will not be ignored.

God always reaches people when they reach the point of desperation. We are a people who have not only lost our nation but have also lost our way. We have laws being written and rewritten that have dismantled virtue, hope, and Christian faith across a generation. As a nation we are the proverbial prop plane that is hopelessly spiraling out of control without any seeming recourse. Legislation, education, and international cooperation cannot and will not pull us out of this nosedive. We desperately need a divine intervention of God, without which the epitaph will read that the plane went down on our watch. We need a holy resuscitation that jump-starts our faith and releases transformative power to our nation. We need a remnant of revivalists who will rise up and take their place.

It is understood that some things remain dormant in us until they are identified and called out. What is needed is for the trumpet to be blown that will summon this epic group and form their core values. (See 1 Corinthians 14:8.)

My personal friend and revivalist Pat Schatzline has done just that in this new book. I found myself riveted by this manuscript—not just intrigued but seriously impacted and inspired to step out of the ordinary course of things. I cannot recall a book that I feel is more significant to this next move of the Spirit than the one you hold in your hands. It's been said, "No harm's done to history by making it something someone would want to read." What you are about to read will be a catalyst to exploits that others will read of you!

I Am Remnant reminds us there is a move of the Spirit that is underway that will release an inbreaking of the kingdom that will create a new breed of believers—a new standard of Christianity—and cause a fresh expression of the church to rise up. God's gift to a nation is an emerging company of remnant revivalists who have a prophetic sense of what heaven is desiring to release and who then step into it. This will not happen without hearing the bell and coming to fight. We didn't start this fight, but we must finish it as heaven puts finishing touches on a masterpiece of redemption through you.

Pat makes the statement, "What you will not fight today will keep you from having authority to confront tomorrow." He then proceeds to give a generation pure, holy nitroglycerin that so explosively ruins the reader for a status quo stroll when a miraculous militant march is urgently needed. This manifesto comes from a seasoned general who has labored for, been broken over, and is a voice to a generation.

I couldn't put this book down, and I know you won't either until you are built into that last-days weaponry that will be God's secret weapon on culture. I highly recommend *I Am Remnant* to anyone who wants to see their faith make a difference and the name of Jesus made famous in a generation. Whether you are young or seasoned, this is the book for you as a remnant whom history and heaven now call out!

—SEAN SMITH

AUTHOR OF *PROPHETIC EVANGELISM* AND *I AM YOUR SIGN*

DIRECTOR OF SSM/POINTBLANK INTL.

www.seansmithministries.com

@revseansmith

FOREWORD

GOD ISN'T LOOKING for the biggest and the best, the most gifted or articulate. He is not after the greatest talent or even the most religious. God passionately pursues the willing—those who will remain true to His Word, captured by His love, and bound to His call. Incredibly enough, in the twenty-first century He still seeks what He sought in the time of Malachi: God is seeking a remnant. A remnant is a piece or part of the original. To be part of a remnant means you are radically identified and connected to the authentic.

This world is desperate to see an authentic church. Sadly, much of the church has far removed itself from the original intent of Jesus. We are called to live our lives in the image of our Savior, but instead many who bear His name look nothing like Him. A remnant church looks and behaves like Jesus. It loves what He loves and hates what He hates. Today the church is often better at entertainment than it is at seeing people endued with power. It is more superficial than supernatural. But make no mistake about it: a remnant church will be a supernatural church. As never before in human history, there is a clear call for the authentic remnant of God to arise.

Pat Schatzline has responded to a holy mandate to write this book. Open your heart and receive every word. This is surely heaven's invitation to us all. May we respond and become the radically reconnected remnant God desires and that this generation desperately needs.

—JIM RALEY

AUTHOR AND LEAD PASTOR OF CALVARY CHRISTIAN CENTER

ORMOND BEACH, FL

INTRODUCTION

ARE YOU REMNANT?

That is the question addressed to you as you journey through this book. Time will tell whether or not you answer yes and choose to stand up and lead.

I write this book not to lecture you but rather to send forth a clarion call to the true remnant to rise up and lead. I greet you today not as a minister, evangelist, or author but as someone who is simply in love with a Savior and King named Jesus. I say this because so often we assign titles to ourselves to create a "legitimacy of voice" for our message, when all that really matters is a continual vertical encounter with God and an upward reach for depth of intimacy. God has called us all to realize our potential, which is not found in man's approval or the cheer of the populace but rather in God's direct contact with our hearts.

There is such a stirring in my heart for a supernatural awakening of God's power to stir all generations in the body of Christ. God has birthed this book in my heart over many seasons of desperation. I believe now is the time to share its message. After all, it was Martin Luther who said, "If you want to change the world, pick up your pen and write."[1]

In the chapters that follow I will share with you the vision God has given me "for such a time as this." I will share with you the idea of remnant and ask if you have the remnant calling. We will survey the landscape of our time and see where the remnant needs to rise. You will gain encouragement for the road ahead.

But before we go all those places together, I want to share with you the remnant manifesto. This manifesto was given to me one day when I went for a walk in preparation to write this book. On that walk I heard the voice of the Lord say, "Son, I have a message for you to deliver. Write down what I am about to share with you."

I feverishly began to take notes on my phone, and I began to weep as God gave me the following mandate for this generation. It is a manifesto for you, and you will see the outworking of this manifesto throughout the book.

The Remnant Manifesto

The remnant has found freedom in the arms of a loving Savior who has not only forgiven their past but also now has authority over their future.

The remnant knows the I Am has now made them His.

The remnant consists of those who feel like failures—the fatherless, the forgotten, and the freedom fighters—whose pedigree is that of a scarred Savior.

The remnant rescues the hurting and defends the fatherless.

The remnant cannot be defined by man's concepts because they find their value in the eyes of a Savior.

The remnant has decided that, at all costs, they will not quit on the One who would not quit on them.

The remnant doesn't stop where they should have died because they know Jesus didn't.

The remnant chooses to let go of past hurts in order to experience the freedom that comes with forgiving and moving forward.

The remnant chooses to leave a life of compromise for the spirit of consecration.

The remnant will not be swayed by the wind of compromise, will not stare into the eyes of revenge, and will not seek the approval of the populace.

The remnant seeks holy justice with a passion for pursuing the fallen asleep with the knowledge of Him who is awakening the dead.

The remnant seeks to gain nothing but always has everything to give.

The remnant declares grace with justice, power with meekness, and joy with accountability.

The remnant has mastered the simple fact that true revival is not a gathering of the saved but a resurrection of the lost.

The remnant are private worshippers with a public voice who seek only the revelation of God's kingdom and not their own empire.

The remnant does not bow to culture but finds culture re-created by their passion for Jesus.

The remnant walks among lost humanity not screaming insults or provoking slander, but invading with light that which has only known darkness.

The remnant includes the apostle with worn-out garments, the smiling prophet, the transparent pastor, the weeping missionary, the teacher with tools in hand, and the servant evangelist.

The remnant understands the fruit of the Spirit is not a salad for a church potluck but rather the diet of a lifetime.

The remnant knows the gifts of the Spirit are not for the evangelical, charismatic, and Pentecostal talent show but rather are weapons of a dying leader who has chosen spirit over flesh and freedom over slavery.

The remnant stands on truth until the shifting sand of compromise slides from underneath their feet to reveal the rock of salvation. The remnant does not walk in fear of man's retribution but rather in fear that man will never know the love of a Savior.

The remnant always clashes with religion because they know, throughout history, religion has always tried to be the noose around the neck of a Holy Spirit movement.

The remnant is not a pulpiteer or public speaker but rather a resuscitator of life to those who have lost breath.

The remnant doesn't need the stage but rather a place to call home to bring a weary guest.

The remnant is satisfied at all times because they hunger and thirst after righteousness—and they shall be filled.

The remnant does not walk in flattering circles but rather in the places where the unknown sojourner must be found.

The remnant says yes to the cross and no to the applause, yes to the altar and no to arrogance, yes to the covenant and no to worldly concepts.

The remnant has chosen to be the least of these to the greatest of them.

The remnant sleeps in peace only when night has dawned in order to strengthen the journey and mission.

The remnant hides in the shadows of intercession only long enough to embody the burden of restoration.

The remnant doesn't mind seclusion, knowing it is where strength is found, as their peace comes from secret encounters and private glances with the heavenly Father.

The remnant has decided that, at all costs, they will not allow the next generation to speak of the last generation as a group that didn't want to see God's glory.

The remnant is afraid of only one thing: that time will not permit all they feel called by God to do.

This book is critical to the life of all believers who are ready to go where few have trod. It is time to rescue, revive, and release the warriors. Many will have scars from hurts and pain, but those are turned into God testimonies. In fact, scars are proof of battle!

One last note: This book has been written as an "open letter" to those who are called to rise up. I believe you are called to this and that God has an invitation with your name on it. Therefore I open each chapter with a salutation to you, the remnant. If you are called to be remnant, you will heed the words of each chapter and what its teaching requires of you. As Jesus said, "Many get invited; only a few make it" (Matt. 22:14).

We must hear a generation young and old shout, "I am remnant!" Get ready for a new declaration of truth over your life.

SECTION I

THE REMNANT MUST RISE

Chapter 1

AN OPEN LETTER TO THE REMNANT

*So too, at the present time there is
a remnant chosen by grace.*

—ROMANS 11:5, NIV

DEAR REMNANT,
   This is your moment to rise up and make your mark.
Destiny is at your door, and it wants to know what history
will say about you. Please realize your freedom requires a
response. Are you up for the challenge to prove God right
and the devil wrong?

> The remnant has decided that, at all costs,
> they will not allow the next generation to
> speak of the last generation as a group
> that didn't want to see God's glory.

I am calling you out. That's right! That's what an open
letter is created to do. I am here to remind you that you—
yes, you—are an open letter to the world. Psalm 139:16 says,
"Like an open book, you watched me grow from conception
to birth; all the stages of my life were spread out before you,
the days of my life all prepared before I'd even lived one day."
God has laid out your days. You must understand this is your
"now" moment.

Do you realize you're not here by chance? God planned

1

you out! He has written the chapters of your life. He has created a voice in you that must be used. You are the voice of truth to a deceived world where confusion and lost purpose reign. You are not an accident or a mistake—God doesn't make mistakes. God takes the ones the world calls nobodies and declares that they are somebodies:

> Hosea put it well: I'll call nobodies and make them somebodies; I'll call the unloved and make them beloved. In the place where they yelled out, "You're nobody!" they're calling you "God's living children."
>
> —Romans 9:25–26

You were not created to just occupy a space but rather to invade this world with the good news. Could it be possible that by the time you finish this book, you will realize this is your "now" moment? You are a letter to the world. That's right! God chose you as His letter:

> You yourselves are all the endorsement we need. Your very lives are a letter that anyone can read by just looking at you. Christ himself wrote it—not with ink, but with God's living Spirit; not chiseled into stone, but carved into human lives—and we publish it.
>
> —2 Corinthians 3:2–3

Spiritual leaders have written open letters throughout history in the hopes that those letters would awaken a nation. Evangelist Billy Graham published one such open letter to America on July 24, 2012, titled "My Heart Aches for America." In it he said:

> Just a few weeks ago in a prominent city in the South, Christian chaplains who serve the police department were ordered to no longer mention the Name of Jesus in prayer. It was reported that during a recent police-sponsored event, the only person allowed to pray

was someone who addressed "the being in the room."
Similar scenarios are now commonplace in towns
across America. Our society strives to avoid any possibility of offending anyone—except God. Yet the farther we get from God, the more the world spirals out
of control. My heart aches for America and its deceived
people. The wonderful news is that our Lord is a God
of mercy, and He responds to repentance. In Jonah's
day, Nineveh was the lone world superpower—wealthy,
unconcerned, and self-centered. When the Prophet
Jonah finally traveled to Nineveh and proclaimed God's
warning, people heard and repented. I believe the same
thing can happen once again, this time in our nation.[1]

I believe the time is now for the awakening of a generation,
just as Billy Graham wrote in his letter, and let me tell you
why I believe this. On February 10, 2012, I was in Modesto,
California, speaking at the Ammunition Youth Conference.
That night a powerful voice in my life, evangelist Reinhard
Bonnke, declared to me, "Pat, we must get a generation filled
with the Spirit. We must see a generation rise up like no
other has ever seen to lead the outpouring that is coming!"

I felt so challenged at that moment, and I began to pray
God would show me how this monumental task could be
achieved. Pastor Bonnke also told me how God will peri-
odically take him to heaven in his dreams and speak with
him. From that night forward I began to pray for prophetic
dreams to happen in my life.

I do not dream very often, and when I do, I rarely remember
details. But late one night in October 2012 I had a very powerful prophetic dream, and this time my ability to remember
my dream was profoundly different. I remembered so many
intricate details.

In the dream I found myself sitting in an old diner at a
table surrounded by great leaders in our nation, including
Reinhard Bonnke. As we sat in this old diner together, I

noticed in front of us on the table a very old radio with large dials. I began to turn the knobs, and when I landed upon a live station, the knobs would light up. I noticed we were all laughing and crying as I turned each channel on the radio because we could hear reports of outpourings of God in cities and towns across the world. The announcer would say things like, "There is an outpouring of God in San Antonio!" I would quickly turn the dial to the next station only to hear, "There is another outbreak in New York City!"

It felt as if the dream went on all night, and we heard the reports on the radio from cities all across the nation. We listened to reports from all over the world of God pouring out His Spirit and our nation being drawn back to Him.

I awakened to find myself weeping and crying out to God. I looked at the clock, expecting it to be around 5:00 a.m., but it was exactly midnight. I jumped out of bed, and my wife, Karen, was awakened by my stirring and asked if everything was OK.

"Karen, the move of God is coming," I told her. "I just saw it in a dream!"

I ran upstairs and wrote Reinhard Bonnke an e-mail, telling him what I had dreamed. I was amazed when he responded a short time later, saying, "I also sense in my spirit that God's time for America is about to break upon us!"

So let me ask you this: Could it be that all God needs to awaken our nation is a remnant to carry out His plan? I believe that is, indeed, all He needs.

One of my heroes of the faith, pastor David Wilkerson, once penned a powerful devotional about God's use of a remnant to accomplish His plans—and especially God's plan to use a remnant in the end times. Here are a few words from that devotional:

> All the prophets saw the end times and prophesied of the gathering of a separated, holy people who would have great understanding in the Word of the Lord.

Daniel heard great things from God but "understood not" (Daniel 12:8). However, he saw a day coming when a purified, tried and tested remnant would understand; there would be a last-day company full of wisdom and discernment in the things of God. "Many shall be purified, and made white, and tried; but the wicked shall do wickedly: and none of the wicked shall understand; but the wise shall understand" (Daniel 12:10).[2]

Are you wondering by now what a remnant is? I'll go into greater detail about this in the next chapter, but for now let me tell you how John Michael Talbot, one of the founding fathers of contemporary Christian music, defined it when speaking to me one day. Today Talbot is a charismatic Catholic leader who feels called to bring Holy Spirit encounters to the Catholic Church, and when I asked him his definition of remnant, he said, "Remnant—it's the people who don't just practice the externals of their faith, but it's the people who know Jesus."

People who don't just practice the externals of their faith, and people who know Jesus. Is this you? Are you, in fact, remnant? Turn the page to see what it will take for the remnant to rise!

Chapter 2

ARE YOU REMNANT?

The seed will grow well, the vine will yield its fruit,
the ground will produce its crops, and the heavens
will drop their dew. I will give all these things as
an inheritance to the remnant of this people.
—ZECHARIAH 8:12, NIV

Dear Remnant,
Are you ready to help clean up this
mess? Creation awaits your arrival, and
you are a rag in the hand of God.

O N SATURDAY, MAY 26, 2012, I went for an early morning
jog. I was preparing my mind and heart for a high
school graduation at Trinity Christian School in Cedar Hill,
Texas. I was the keynote speaker that day to a crowd of more
than two thousand people.

My mind also weighed heavy for my next assignment in
Houston, Texas. Following the graduation, I would leave
immediately and drive down to Houston to speak at a large
gathering of over forty churches at Christian Temple Church
for Pentecost Sunday—the Sunday that falls fifty days after
Easter and celebrates the outpouring of God found in Acts
2:4. Pastor Don Nordin, who was leading the event, told me
the churches attending the service were very hungry for an
outpouring of God.

I knew in my heart these were not two different assignments, but rather they intersected in the Spirit. One service had students climbing the stairs of a stage to receive a diploma that marked the next chapter of their young lives, and the other service observed a time when 120 young believers climbed the stairs to the Upper Room and waited on God to send the promise of the Holy Spirit.

As I was jogging, I began to pray in the Spirit. Suddenly I heard the voice of the Lord say to me, "Pat, I am looking for the remnant rising!"

When I heard those words, my curiosity drove me back to my hotel room to research the word *remnant*. As I researched, prayed, and researched some more, I began to realize this was the answer to the awakening I believe is coming to the world. This was an answer to the challenge I'd received from Reinhard Bonnke!

Here is what I found when I researched the word *remnant*:

1. Dictionary.com defines it as "remaining, what is left over, usually small part, a fragment or scrap, unsold or unused piece of cloth, as at the end of a bolt."

2. In the Bible the word for *remnant* is the same definition in the Old and New Testaments. In Hebrew the word is *sha'ar*, and in Greek the word is *leimma*. Here is the biblical meaning: "What remains of a group of people after most of that group has been destroyed or lost through dispersal brought upon by judgment or the following of apostasy."[1]

In other words, a remnant is a rag in the hand of God, waiting to be used to clean up the mess. The world is certainly a mess, isn't it? And we who are remnant are God's towel that He uses to clean up lives and transform this world.

As the definition also indicates, a remnant is that which is found at the end of a bolt of cloth. The bolt is the cardboard or wooden spindle or roll that the cloth is attached to for shipment to a store. The remnant on that bolt is the very last little piece that no one wants after the bigger pieces have been sold. Those who use the remnants of a bolt of cloth usually make very small articles of clothing, toys, or quilts. The smallest, seemingly least useful piece of cloth is used with other remnants of cloth to be woven into something beautiful that provides warmth. So, when the remnant comes together, it is comprised of people who are beautiful to the Creator and provide the warmth and comfort of the gospel in the midst of the confusion of this world.

> The remnant knows the I AM
> has now made them His.

Lastly, the remnant is the group that has always stood firm in times where truth was absent.

All of these truths should make you shout! You are not here by chance. In fact, long before a pregnancy test declared you would be coming into this world, God had already planned for your arrival. You were not a shock to God, but my prayer is that you will shock the forces of hell with your tenacity, passion, and hunger for all things God—that is, if you are remnant.

Are you remnant?

THE LEGACY OF THE REMNANT

This idea of a remnant is nothing new. For thousands of years Satan has tried to destroy the very foundation God has laid for us, and when you study the Old Testament, the Bible speaks over and over of remnants that remained after the great massacres of God's people. It also speaks of those who were called to be separated and to stand during wicked times. Look what Isaiah wrote in Isaiah 10:21: "A remnant will return, a remnant of Jacob will return to the Mighty God" (NIV).

The *Holman Bible Dictionary* says, "The remnant doctrine was so important to Isaiah that he named one of his sons Shear-Jashub, meaning 'A Remnant Shall Return' (Isaiah 7:3). Isaiah would write about how the faithful would survive the onslaughts of the Assyrian army (Isaiah 4:2–6; Isaiah 12:1–6) as illustrated by the remarkable deliverance of the few people in Jerusalem from the siege of the city by the Assyrians (Isaiah 36–38)."[2]

Peter Leithart, in his commentary on 1 and 2 Kings, tells us more about this remnant prophecy given by Isaiah: "This prophecy of a coming remnant was given to a godly and just king named Hezekiah by the Prophet Isaiah. King Hezekiah was the king of Judah, and during his reign he had tore down idols and restored the house of God. In II Kings 19 the kingdom is under siege by the Assyrians and its evil King Sennacherib. As Hezekiah watched his nation being destroyed, he went into the temple to pray to God for help (II Kings 19:15). No other king had done that in over 250 years."[3]

As Hezekiah despaired Judah being destroyed, the prophet Isaiah sent him this prophetic promise: "Once more a remnant of the kingdom of Judah will take root below and bear fruit above. For out of Jerusalem will come a remnant, and out of Mount Zion a band of survivors. The zeal of the LORD Almighty will accomplish this" (2 Kings 19:30–31, NIV).

The prophet Isaiah prophesied the restoration of the remnant of Israel—those who would stand when others would take a bow to culture and desires of flesh. They are the "fraternity of the remnant." In the worst of times they still held the belief that God could do anything and use anyone He wanted.

THE TIME IS NOW

It is time to assign a similar biblical identity to this generation. As God has raised up remnants at critical moments throughout history, they have been marked with the Nazirite (consecrated) vow of holiness, wholeness, and purpose. They have chosen to overcome the flesh for a greater call to consecration. They have decided to be a drink offering rather than host a bar tab.

There is a similar prophetic mantle on this generation. I hear the voice of Jesus calling out for the voices of truth to rise. And to get where God wants us to go, we must be God-empowered and not platform-driven. Without purity we will only embarrass the cross. Without authority we will never see miracles. Without joy our message will be ignored. I must remind you that Jesus came with a sword and not a feather!

Those two services I led in May 2012 marked my heart in a profound way. I found myself wondering: Why could we not see a mighty move of God at a high school graduation? What will it take to see this generation climb the stairs of the Upper Room? For years I have often wondered and have even said during private conversations with my wife, "Will we ever see the outpouring of God?"

The powerful prophecy given in Joel 2 for today says, "And afterward, I will pour out my Spirit on all people. Your sons and daughters will prophesy, your old men will dream dreams, your young men will see visions. Even on my servants, both men and women, I will pour out my Spirit in those days" (vv. 28–29, NIV). The great New Testament pastor Simon Peter declared this message of Joel's on the Day of Pentecost in Acts 2. But when will we see its fulfillment? Why haven't we seen it yet?

I do believe it will happen in my lifetime, but it will require a remnant to rise up. Maybe I am a foolish dreamer to believe this, but foolish dreamers are the inventors of the next level. I have always been a dreamer—in fact, that goes along with all of my report cards in middle school, upon which my teachers nearly always wrote in the comment area, "Pat daydreams too much." Once a teacher wrote a message that has stuck with me through the years. Writing on the back of one of my six-week report cards, she said, "Pat seems to always be in any location besides the classroom mentally!" I am not sure what I was thinking about to cause my teachers to write such things—most likely I was thinking about sports or girls or planning my next adventure that would surely end in a visit to the principal's office.

And though I certainly learned to focus eventually, I still find myself daydreaming today—only my dreams have changed. I now dream of a generation running to the altar and experiencing God. I dream of the day when the glory of the Lord will invade our services, conferences, and gatherings.

My daydreams have also turned to night dreams, and recently I had another dream that has stayed with me. In the dream I saw the feet of Jesus. Then I heard Him say to me, "Pat, if you will give Me everything you have, I will give you everything I have. Pat, tell this generation that if they will give Me everything they have, I will give them everything I have."

I awoke from the dream and realized I was weeping and shaking in my sleep.

So, why do we need a remnant, and why do we need it now?

> The remnant sleeps in peace only when night has dawned in order to strengthen the journey and mission.

Here's why. We are living in desperate times. We now live not only in a time that encompasses false teachers and the growth of false religions, but also in a time when much masquerades as Christianity. Some preachers of the gospel now teach there is no need for conviction or repentance. We are living in a time when grace is abused and purity is considered an old term. We are living in a time when freedom in the Spirit is relegated to a quarterly retreat and authority is demanded without a spiritual father's blessing. It is a time when the apostolic has been diminished by an entrepreneurial approach to church growth. It is a day where truth has been replaced by relevance to culture and the demand for a message without conviction.

And yet I share all of this with great excitement. Why? Because I believe that if these are desperate times, then we are positioned for a great awakening. Desperation has and always will be the birthplace of miracles. God has raised up small groups of what I call the nobodies—the leftovers, the counted out, and the unqualified throughout history that He chose "for such a time as this" who understood it was their moment to rise up and lead.

God has not forgotten us. He will raise up His remnant! If He did it for King Hezekiah, He will do it for us. We must get back to the house of God and cry out for such deliverance.

God is not done with our nation. He is calling out to those who will invite Him in. Revelation 3:20 states, "Here I am! I stand at the door and knock. If anyone hears my voice and opens the door, I will come in and eat with him, and he with me" (NIV). Jesus declared He was standing outside the door, knocking, waiting to be let in to His church.

This has many implications. It may mean not allowing the clock to be in control anymore. It may mean laying down our order of services. It certainly means calling the church back to intimacy with God as we have never seen. Programs are important for the foundation of a church, but there are times when programs dictate the desperation level.

The apostle Paul said, "So too, at the present time there is a remnant chosen by grace" (Rom. 11:5, NIV). And the reality is, Paul lived in a time very much like today. It was a time when many had rejected the Messiah and decided to follow the philosophy of man. Poets were spouting hedonism and humanism not just as entertainment but also as dogma and truth. It was also a very dangerous time, where Christians were being persecuted and martyred by Rome and the Jewish religious leaders. Anyone who claimed to be a believer in Christ faced certain torture and death.

What many do not realize is that it is still very dangerous to be a Christian. Since AD 33 more than 70 million Christians have been martyred for their faith, and it is believed that four hundred a day die for the cause of Christ.[4] The apostle Paul was saying to the very young New Testament church—and to us, today, who follow Christ—that God has you. You are on His radar.

We are a remnant chosen by grace. I am amazed at how those powerful words resonate with today's Christians. And so you have to ask yourself this question: *Am I remnant?* Through the next few chapters I hope you can answer yes.

Chapter 3

AN AUDIENCE OF ONE

This is what the LORD Almighty says: "It
may seem marvelous to the remnant of this
people at that time, but will it seem marvelous
to me?" declares the LORD Almighty.

—ZECHARIAH 8:6, NIV

Dear Remnant,
Check your spiritual mailbox! There
is a letter from the One who knows you
best sitting in the secret chamber of your
heart. God has sent you an invitation to
have an audience with Him. He desires
an encounter with His child—and that
child is you.

ACH YEAR AT the beginning of the summer my family
heads to the beach for a time of fun and rest. It's a
time I also use to prepare my heart and mind for a long
summer of ministry all over the nation. One morning in
the summer of 2012 I came into our rented condo after an
early morning time of jogging and asked my daughter, Abby,
where Mommy was. She told me she was out on the balcony
of the condo.

I started to walk through the door to the balcony when I
saw Karen having her morning devotions. Just as I went to

step through the door, I heard the Spirit of God say to me, "Don't bother her—she is having an audience of one!"

I sheepishly headed back inside and joined Abby on the couch. Karen was having her private time with her Savior, and the last thing she needed was for me to interrupt. But honestly, I was a little bit jealous and a little bit convicted. I had not had a deep encounter with God in a while. This moment stirred me to go and spend time with God. (My wife has always had the ability to push me closer to God just by her relationship with Jesus!)

I share this with you because I believe it is possible to get so wrapped up in ministry that you forget the power of God's presence. This is so dangerous. When you forget to spend time with God, you can become a slave to mechanical ministry. If you're not careful, you begin to preach, teach, or lead without firsthand knowledge of what God is saying.

YOUR EXCLUSIVE INVITATION

Imagine walking out to your mailbox one afternoon, reaching into the box, and pulling out a beautiful invitation. It is marked private, and it is a summons from a king—not just any king, but the King of kings Himself.

This isn't any ordinary invitation, either. The invitation is made with the finest paper you have ever held. Excitement overwhelms you as you start to open the envelope. The invitation is sealed with a majestic clay seal. You slowly break open the seal and pull out the card. It says, "You are hereby invited to an audience of One." As you read on, you realize this is an invitation to leave the busyness of the world—to go past the noise of the culture, the voices of despair, the growls of the pundits, the whining of the disenchanted, the gasps of the religious, and the roars of the ambitious—and go back to a place where all that matters is those in attendance: you and your King.

Before I can take you deeper into the understanding

of remnant, I must challenge you to seek out and maintain such an audience of One. I spent years trying to lead without a guide, years trying to be a man without listening to the Father—years walking as a failure. But then I had an encounter with the Messiah, the One, and I am now convinced that if a person ever has an encounter with the one true God, it will transform him or her forever.

> The remnant doesn't mind seclusion,
> knowing it is where strength is
> found, as their peace comes from
> secret encounters and private
> glances with the heavenly Father.

I always enjoy seeing God pour out His Spirit in church services, conferences, and large gatherings, but God also desires to spend one-on-one time with His creation. In fact, God's Word promises that we are fulfilled in His presence: "You make known to me the path of life; you will fill me with joy in your presence, with eternal pleasures at your right hand" (Ps. 16:11, NIV). Did you know God is always ready to wrap His arms around you? In fact, you were created for God's pleasure: "You created everything, and it is for your pleasure that they exist and were created" (Rev. 4:11, NLT [1996]).

Remnant, you must understand that such private encounters with God are the bloodline of healthy Christians. Those encounters with your Savior are what keep you spiritually alive. Look at how the psalmist put it in Psalm 18:6: "A hostile world! I call to GOD, I cry to God to help me. From his palace he hears my call; my cry brings me right into his presence—a private audience!"

God wants an audience with you. And I have learned that if the devil can't make you sin, then he will just make you busy. Why? Because God can do more in you than life can ever take from you. Show me a person who worships in private, and I will show you someone who needs very little advice. It is in your private time with Jesus that peace and contentment come to every aspect of your life. This is critical to your walk. Jesus said in Matthew 5:5, "You're blessed when you're content with just who you are—no more, no less. That's the moment you find yourselves proud owners of everything that can't be bought." It is during those private, one-on-one moments that Jesus secures you and transforms you.

LIVE IN GOD-TIME

When God comes near, it changes everything. It is as if time stands still. I call this a *kairos* moment. What is a *kairos* moment? It is a God-timed moment.

We live our lives using chronological clocks. That is called *chronos* time. But God's timing is very different: "Kairos (καιρός) is an ancient Greek word meaning the right or opportune moment (the supreme moment). The ancient Greeks had two words for time, chronos and kairos. While the former refers to chronological or sequential time, the latter signifies a time between, a moment of indeterminate time in which something special happens. What the special something is depends on who is using the word. While chronos is quantitative, kairos has a qualitative nature."[1]

The Bible speaks of our time on earth in both time periods— our regular life span of years (*chronos*) and our time on earth that God has planned out (*kairos*). In other words, God sees you in two time zones. This is a powerful thought, because it means that during your normal days, God can interject a "God moment"—a moment that interrupts everything—at any time. Suddenly your life comes into focus and you experience transformation.

I have often said there are about fifteen minutes of

revelation in your whole life. They are the stringing together of hundreds, if not thousands, of *kairos* moments. I personally would not even want to live without them. Those moments have transformed everything about me. They are supernatural encounter moments—times God has already penciled in His heavenly day planner to mess me up in the best of ways.

The deeper we go with God, the more it ruins us. But we must let God move us in this way. As Sir Francis Drake said, "Disturb us, Lord, when we are too well pleased with ourselves, when our dreams have come true because we dreamed too little, when we arrive safely because we have sailed too close to the shore. Disturb us, Lord..."[2]

This happened to me at sixteen years of age, when God walked into my bedroom late one night and radically changed me. During this time of my life I was a long way off from having a real relationship with God. I had begun to experiment with alcohol, and I was a terrible influence on my friends. I found that I could not sleep. I was at a crossroads in my life. I had seen the good and the bad of ministry after being raised in a minister's home. There was a deep cry in my spirit for God to be real, and I had decided that if He was not, then I was done with Christianity. I knew that I couldn't live in my parents' revelation of God anymore. I had an unrest in me, and I knew there had to be more to life.

One night I could not sleep, and I decided to crawl out of bed and lie on the floor. Throughout my life I had seen my dad do that. I would get up in the night to get a glass of water and see him lying on the floor in the family room praying. I thought I would give it a try. I had never done that before and wondered if God would come and visit me in my basement bedroom in Oneonta, Alabama. As I began to pray, I felt nothing.

After a while I got sleepy and began to doze off. Then suddenly I felt the presence of God in my room. I began to look around to see if I could see God. I said, "God, if You are real, then speak to me! I need You to speak!" I suddenly heard the voice of God say, "Pat, I love you! I have a plan for your life!" Then God said something that was transformational to me. He said, "Pat, I am sorry you have seen things in My church that have hurt you, but if you will follow Me, I will use you to heal people!" This was my first *kairos* moment! Did I get completely free at that moment? No! But that began the journey that led me to freedom.

All through the Bible we see these *kairos* moments:

- Moses had a powerful *kairos* moment as God walked by and he saw God's hinder parts (Exod. 33–34).

- Abraham experienced many *kairos* moments as he walked with God (Gen. 17–22).

- Jacob experienced a *kairos* moment as he wrestled with God (Gen. 32).

- David understood these *kairos* moments, as he wrote about them in the Psalms: "One day spent in your house, this beautiful place of worship, beats thousands spent on Greek island beaches. I'd rather scrub floors in the house of my God than be honored as a guest in the palace of sin" (Ps. 84:10).

- John the Baptist had a *kairos* moment when he met Jesus and declared, "I have seen and I testify that this is the Son of God" (John 1:34, NIV).

- The disciples had a *kairos* moment when Jesus walked up to them and called them to follow Him.

- The woman at the well had a supernatural moment when Jesus spoke to her: "It's who you are and the way you live that count before God.

Your worship must engage your spirit in the pursuit of truth. That's the kind of people the Father is out looking for: those who are simply and honestly themselves before him in their worship. God is sheer being itself—Spirit. Those who worship him must do it out of their very being, their spirits, their true selves, in adoration" (John 4:23–24).

- The woman with the issue of blood had one of these moments when she touched Jesus's robe (Luke 8:43–44).

- Simon Peter felt such *kairos* time when the hand of Jesus stretched out to grab him as he sank into the water (Matt. 14).

- Saul, who later became the apostle Paul, had a *kairos* moment when he fell to the dirt and saw Jesus on the road to Damascus (Acts 9).

- The apostle John experienced a long and deep *kairos* moment on a deserted island called Patmos, where he wrote the Book of Revelation.

Kairos moments are the supernatural God interruptions of your now that forever change your future. They can be experienced in visions, in dreams, or simply through the overwhelming power of God's Spirit entering a room. They are invitations for you to have an audience of one—and not just anyone, but *the One*.

WILL YOU WALK INTO THE ROOM?

We must get closer to the One, as God's Word declares: "Come near to God and he will come near to you. Wash your hands, you sinners, and purify your hearts, you double-minded" (James 4:8, NIV). Who is this One we are called to get closer to? The One knocking at the door of hearts, churches, and cities: "Look at me. I stand at the door. I knock. If you hear me call and open the door, I'll come right in and sit down to supper with you. Conquerors will sit alongside me at the head table, just as I, having conquered, took the place of honor at the side of my Father. That's my gift to the conquerors!" (Rev. 3:20–21).

God says He has a place waiting for you, and that place is right beside Him. He can fix a broken heart. He can heal a marriage. He can change a broken man into a warrior. He can grab the heart of a teenager and make him or her secure. He can speak things like, "Go to China and rescue your daughter," as He did to our family. He can speak to you to start a business, go to college, or simply go to prayer.

Do you understand that without Jesus we can't produce anything anyway? In John 15 He teaches, "I am the Vine, you are the branches. When you're joined with me and I with you, the relation intimate and organic, the harvest is sure to be abundant. Separated, you can't produce a thing. Anyone who separates from me is deadwood, gathered up and thrown on the bonfire. But if you make yourselves at home with me and my words are at home in you, you can be sure that whatever you ask will be listened to and acted upon" (vv. 5–7).

If we are joined with Jesus, we are promised the ability to rebuild what has been destroyed: "You'll use the old rubble of past lives to build anew, rebuild the foundations from out of your past. You'll be known as those who can fix anything, restore old ruins, rebuild and renovate, make the community livable again" (Isa. 58:12). This is essential for the remnant, for this is our calling—to repair, to restore, to bring back that which has been cast off.

To fulfill this remnant calling, are you willing to walk into the room where God is? Walk past those with fainted hearts, low expectations, and religious disbelief. Walk past the rowdy false interpreters and legalists and get yourself to the Savior. He is in the room! Look past everyone else.

This is what happened when Mary walked into Simon's house in Mark 14. Jesus was sitting in the house being grilled by the Pharisees when Mary did something so absorbed. She walked past everyone and broke her alabaster box on the floor. Then she began to anoint Jesus in front of everyone. This girl with a broken past had broken her perfume box, and she did it on purpose because she loved her King.

This was not a friendly room. It was a room full of winks and nods. It was a room full of judgment. The Pharisees were intent on tricking Jesus, and no one wanted this woman there. But Mary knew she had to anoint her King for His death. She was in a crowded room, but she had an audience of One. It was a *kairos* moment.

The people in the room, including Judas, began to rebuke her, but Jesus challenged them on her behalf: "Leave her alone! Why are you bothering her?" In other words, when you have an audience of One, God will have your back. He will stand up for you. In fact, Jesus went on to say that Mary's actions would be remembered forever: "I tell you the truth, wherever the gospel is preached throughout the world, what she has done will also be told, in memory of her" (Mark 14:9, NIV).

Mary would have another powerful transformation—a *kairos* moment—in the garden when Jesus resurrected (John 20:14–16). Because of her obedience, she got a front row seat to the resurrection of the King. In fact, her testimony of the resurrection would be used throughout history to tell the world, "Jesus is risen!"

Just imagine what could happen when you make an audience of One your priority too. Who knows what stories will be told of you in the decades and centuries to come?

Four Places That Lead You
to an Audience of One

Want to know how to get to that room—how to secure that audience of One? God can bring it before you a number of ways. Here are four places in your life that will lead you straight there.

1. The place of frustration

I have learned God will allow you to get frustrated. He will push you to a place of transformation through that frustration. When you are frustrated and desperate for change, that's when God loves to shows up. You will begin to cry that it is time for change—and that's when God will bring it.

> For the creation was subjected to frustration, not by its own choice, but by the will of the one who subjected it, in hope that the creation itself will be liberated from its bondage to decay and brought into the glorious freedom of the children of God.
> —Romans 8:20–21, niv

I'm usually frustrated with winter by the time spring comes, but what keeps me going during the seasons is knowing the seasons always change. Have you ever needed an encounter, not just information? I have, and it's usually at my lowest points in life—when I have done everything I can do and finally relinquish it all to God. That's when I hear His voice.

Your frustration is a sign that God has something huge waiting for you. Sometimes God will allow you to become frustrated in order to open your eyes to the truth of your need for Him. If life was always comfortable, we would never move to the next level, and we would miss our moment.

2. The place of desperation

When God is allowed to take control of your life, He will take you from frustration to desperation.

When I was desperate, I called out, and GOD got me out of a tight spot. GOD's angel sets up a circle of protection around us while we pray.

—PSALM 34:6–7

We are living in desperate times. Nations are rising against nations. Earthquakes and tsunamis are ravaging the earth. Divorce and suicide are at an all-time high. Voices of confusion and humanism infiltrate at every level. People are searching for answers, but we never keep quiet long enough to hear God speak.

But hear this: God loves desperate people!

Desperate, I throw myself on you: you are my God!

—PSALM 31:14

My desperation has left me speechless many times, which opened the door for God to speak. There is not a jail or prison created on earth that can keep God out. He will walk right through the prison doors of your life:

A hard sentence, and your hearts so heavy, and not a soul in sight to help. Then you called out to God in your desperate condition; he got you out in the nick of time. He led you out of your dark, dark cell, broke open the jail and led you out. So thank GOD for his marvelous love, for his miracle mercy to the children he loves; He shattered the heavy jailhouse doors, he snapped the prison bars like matchsticks!

—PSALM 107:12–16

God is looking for people who simply desire Him above everything else. No matter what state you're in, He can reach in and pull you out.

3. The place of confrontation
Don't complain about what you're not willing to confront. A moment has to arise where you're willing to confront what has

held you back. Jeremiah said, "After those years of running loose, I repented. After you trained me to obedience, I was ashamed of my past, my wild, unruly past. Humiliated, I beat on my chest. Will I ever live this down?" (Jer. 31:19).

We must let go of our past in order to see our future. Our past can become our crutch to remaining a victim. You must declare, "No more!" Then God will strengthen your heart to take you to the next level of freedom. As 1 Thessalonians 3:13 says, "May he strengthen your hearts so that you will be blameless and holy in the presence of our God and Father when our Lord Jesus comes with all his holy ones" (NIV).

If we allow God to confront us now, then we will be freed from a terrible future. Paul said, "Better to be confronted by the Master now than to face a fiery confrontation later" (1 Cor. 11:32). Jesus is all about confrontation. He loves you enough to get into your stuff. He said, "Do you think I came to smooth things over and make everything nice? Not so. I've come to disrupt and confront!" (Luke 12:51). God never called us to be comfortable!

4. The place of revelation

Finally, there is a moment in every person's life where they have to become the one who experiences the encounter with God. This is the *kairos* moment. And the place where you suddenly have an encounter is the place where you receive God's revelation and love. The disciple John said, "How great is the love the Father has lavished on us, that we should be called children of God! And that is what we are!" (1 John 3:1, NIV). As my wife, Karen, always says, "If a generation will catch one glimpse of the Father, it will transform them forever." It is time to catch the glimpse of the Father.

I am convinced that if you get ahold of this message, it will set you free. You will finally know who you are! This is the way the woman at the well must have felt. This is the way the small children Jesus called to Himself must have felt. This is the way Lazarus must have felt when he exited his tomb. This is the way

Peter must have felt when he felt the hand of God as he sank in the water. This is the way Mary and John must have felt when Jesus looked at them from the cross. I am talking about a personal encounter with God.

God is calling you to such an encounter! If you're frustrated, if you're desperate, if you're ready to confront, if you're ready for a revelation of the Father's love, if you don't fit in—this is your moment. He is ready to transform you. Revelation always leads to transformation, and your acceptance of the invitation means you are getting closer to being remnant!

Chapter 4

THE TANGLED AND TORN GENERATION

Who is a God like you, who pardons sin and
forgives the transgression of the remnant
of his inheritance? You do not stay angry
forever but delight to show mercy.

—MICAH 7:18, NIV

Dear Remnant,
All of us are wrapped in the chains of
memories, hurts, and disappointments.
The question is: Will you rise above and
turn the pain into power for God? That
is what the remnant does! Your influence
starts when you start over. Your freedom
is a declaration to the world that freedom
starts with an encounter with God.

I MUST WARN YOU this chapter is very intense. This is the
chapter where you must really decide if you will take the
first steps toward becoming remnant. This chapter will challenge you, but hopefully it will bring you freedom.

And that's the real crux of it: my goal is for you to realize
all of us must get free. There are consequences unseen if
we choose to not do this—and the greatest of those consequences is the souls that will never be transformed by having

come into contact with the free you. Your freedom determines the freedom of those you are called to encounter and influence.

True freedom comes from acknowledging that the person who stares at you in the mirror deserves to be unwrapped. You are worthy of a life of purpose. The moment you realize you are remnant, you step into the process of rising past your circumstances and hurts. Your purpose then becomes the road others can take to that same freedom.

It's Time to Fly Free

According to Romans 3:23, we have all made mistakes. We all have scars from our past that continually try to dictate our future. We must quit wrestling with whether or not the cross is powerful enough to handle our mistakes and sin. Somewhere along the way we must decide to turn our backs on the world's concepts and identities.

> The remnant consists of those who feel like failures—the fatherless, the forgotten, and the freedom fighters—whose pedigree is that of a scarred Savior.

Let me illustrate this for you with a story about my son, Nate. Today Nate is a youth pastor in Cedar Hill, Texas, and he does an amazing job with hundreds of students at Trinity Church and Explicit Youth Ministries. But in Nate's senior year of high school he entered a season of amazing struggle. He was preparing to play football in college, but the pressure he was under was extremely intense. It seemed the enemy was going to do his best to stop Nate in his tracks.

During that senior year he made some very bad decisions. Nate made these decisions over a period of about three months, and he will tell you to this day that he walked down a path God did not have for him.

Afterward those mistakes haunted him nearly every day. We would pray together, but he just couldn't seem to find freedom. After he went off to college, the guilt of the past nearly derailed him.

One day he called me in unbelievable turmoil. He was sitting in his truck at his university, and he was weeping. "Dad," he said, "I just can't get over the guilt of my past. Every day it's all I can think about!"

I wanted so badly to be in Texas with him at that moment. I prayed for God to show me what to do. And what took place next could only have been inspired by the Holy Spirit. In fact, Nate now uses it as part of his personal testimony to change lives.

As Nate sat weeping on the other end of the line, I felt God telling me to have Nate shut his eyes. I said, "Nate, imagine you're standing on the edge of a very high mountain cliff. Now step off the cliff!" Then I said, "Nate, are you falling?"

He said, "I am falling, Dad!" He was weeping uncontrollably at this point.

I said, "Nate, flap your arms! Nate, flap your arms!" I then asked him, "Are you doing it?"

He said, "Yes, sir, I am flapping!"

At this point I began to shout loudly the truth of Isaiah 40:31—that we shall mount up with wings as eagles. "It is time for you to soar! It is time for you to fly past your old life," I said. "Nate, are you flying yet?"

He said, "Dad, I am flying!"

Through the tears we were sharing, I told him to fly over the places where he made mistakes. I told him to fly over the places he visited from his past—places where friends and relationships lived. I asked him, "Can you see their houses?"

Nate said, "I see those places—they are right below me!"

I said, "Keep flying! Are you past them yet?"

Within a few seconds Nate said, "Dad, they are gone. I have flown past them!"

We wept together, and that day freedom came into Nate's life. Literally, the enemy lost his grip on my son. He is now remnant! And he has since walked others through what he walked through. Why? Because once you experience freedom, you have to give it away.

This is the same reason Simon Peter got up and preached on the Day of Pentecost. Remember, just fifty-three days before that, he had become one of the utmost traitors to Jesus. Yet even though he had cursed, shunned, and rejected Jesus, he had a God encounter in the Upper Room (Acts 2:4) that changed everything. It all started with Jesus meeting him on the shore in John 21. Jesus interrupted Peter's despair by cooking him breakfast. Then He said to Peter, "Do you love Me? If you love Me, feed My lambs!" (See John 21:15–17.) This moment let Peter know that even though he had failed miserably, Jesus could still use him.

I challenge you today to shut your eyes and fly past your old mistakes. Fly past your regrets. God has a wide-open horizon awaiting you. Fly into your destiny and leave the old behind. That is what remnant does!

Undone and Untangled

The enemy wants to wrap you up in lies of condemnation, but God has called you to get untangled from this world. You were not created to fit in! John 15 declares that we are called to be separate and not a part of this world: "If you find the godless world is hating you, remember it got its start hating me. If you lived on the world's terms, the world would love you as one of its own. But since I picked you to live on God's terms and no longer on the world's terms, the world is going to hate you" (vv. 18–19).

God's Word also tells us we are called to be different. That is what being remnant is all about. But in order to be remnant, we must untangle ourselves from this world. The world can suffocate the breath of God out of your life, but this world is not our home:

> Friends, this world is not your home, so don't make yourselves cozy in it. Don't indulge your ego at the expense of your soul. Live an exemplary life among the natives so that your actions will refute their prejudices. Then they'll be won over to God's side and be there to join in the celebration when He arrives.
>
> —1 PETER 2:11–12

Let me tell you more about this idea of being set apart and untangled. One morning I was praying as I was getting ready to speak at an event. I kept hearing one particular word as I was praying—the word *undone*. I am not sure why I kept hearing that same word over and over again, but I was a bit weary in Spirit, having ministered a great deal over that period of time.

I had read the word *undone* before in the Bible, but I never really understood it. I knew it was found in Isaiah 6, where Isaiah describes his vision of heaven:

> In the year that King Uzziah died, [in a vision] I saw the Lord sitting upon a throne, high and lifted up, and the skirts of His train filled the [most holy part of the] temple. Above Him stood the seraphim; each had six wings: with two [each] covered his [own] face, and with two [each] covered his feet, and with two [each] flew. And one cried to another and said, Holy, holy, holy is the Lord of hosts; the whole earth is full of His glory! And the foundations of the thresholds shook at the voice of him who cried, and the house was filled with smoke. Then said I, Woe is me! For I am *undone* and ruined, because I am a man of unclean lips, and I

dwell in the midst of a people of unclean lips; for my
eyes have seen the King, the Lord of hosts!

—ISAIAH 6:1–5, AMP, EMPHASIS ADDED

After I remembered it was spoken of in this passage, I
decided to go deeper in my study of the word—and I learned it
is a powerful word with so much meaning. In Hebrew the word
for "undone" is *damah*. Check out the meaning: "to be dumb
or silent; hence, to fail or perish; translated to destroy: cease, be
cut down (off), destroy, be brought to silence, be undone [from
past], utterly [reduced]."[1]

In modern terms, I believe the word means *untangled*.
And that is exactly what this generation needs to be in order
to be remnant.

We are all products of our history. I am always amazed that
what takes place in the early years of our life has the power to
control the later years—the years that really count. We must,
therefore, get a generation into the presence of God so they
can be undone. Undone from their fears. Undone from their
hurt. Undone from their mistakes. Most of all, undone in
God's presence. The end of oneself is the beginning of God.

I am talking about having such a deep encounter with
God that God literally untangles us from our past. Could it
be this is what happened to Isaiah? I have always focused
on how cool the scenery was for him—the angels swarming,
the threshold bouncing up and down, the glory of God all
around. Wow! It's like a scene out of a science fiction movie!

But there is so much more to this powerful God encounter.
Look what it says in Isaiah verse 5:

Then said I, Woe is me! for I am undone; because I
am a man of unclean lips, and I dwell in the midst of
a people of unclean lips: for mine eyes have seen the
King, the LORD of hosts.

—ISAIAH 6:5, KJV

Here is Isaiah, having this unbelievably passionate moment, and he screams out, "Woe is me!" What is it that brought Isaiah to such a place of being undone?

For context, we know he had just experienced the death of his dear friend King Uzziah. (See 2 Chronicles 26.) Uzziah was a great king and leader until he became full of the pride that led to his demise. Then he was struck with leprosy and banished from the house of the Lord. This crushed Isaiah. He loved King Uzziah. So now Isaiah was on a journey of discovery.

Isaiah realized he had entered the presence of God while he was unclean. It forced him to declare, "Undo me! Ruin me!" He was shouting, "Start me over! Take me back to where I began! Remove my regrets and redeem me! Make me whole! I am desperate!"

It's just as Paul declares in 2 Corinthians 5:17:

> Now we look inside, and what we see is that anyone united with the Messiah gets a fresh start, is created new. The old life is gone; a new life burgeons!

Isaiah had a deep and powerful confrontation. The confrontation wasn't with injustice, religion, or lack. So many times we blame the end results instead of dealing with the root. When Isaiah walked into the throne room, in essence he was alone. Yes, there were angels flying all around him, making declarations of God's presence, and yes, God Himself was in the room. But what really mattered is that Isaiah showed up to church that day—and he was by himself!

Isaiah was at the end of himself. He needed a transformation moment. And he experienced a personal encounter with God. I have never met anyone who represents the remnant who did not first have a powerful encounter with God. It is a life-altering moment that changes them forever—and it changes the lives of those around them too.

For instance, my dad was a drug dealer in Detroit. One night he cried out to Jesus, and he had an encounter. It all started with a man named John who lived in our neighbor-hood. John was a gregarious fellow with no front teeth, and he was radical about Jesus. He had knocked on the door of our home and continually invited us to church. My father couldn't stand him. In fact, my father threatened over and over to knock out the rest of his teeth if he kept bothering our family. But one evening my mother went to church with John's family and gave her heart to Christ. For the next couple of weeks my dad wrestled with what happened to my mom. She was different. Jesus had changed her.

One night my dad finally came to the end of himself. He knelt on the bathroom floor, flushed his drugs down the commode, and cried out to God for salvation. That encounter changed my family lineage. Never again would our family be the same. Within six months my parents would pack us all up in an old station wagon and move us from Detroit to Colorado Springs, Colorado, where my dad enrolled in Bible college. That one night started my entire family on a journey that is still at work in our lives today.

The Importance of Moving Forward

Freedom begins and ends at the cross. Jesus was crucified between two thieves, and I believe those thieves represent yesterday and tomorrow. Yesterday has the power to steal your joy because of your past, and a fear of tomorrow can keep you from dreaming. Why? Because Satan wants your past and your future—but Jesus stands in your today! If Jesus is in your today, then all worry and fear must leave. As Oswald Chambers once said, "Leave the broken, irreversible past in God's hands, and step out into the invincible future with Him."[2]

The writer of Hebrews helps us realize our need to move forward:

> Therefore then, since we are surrounded by so great a
> cloud of witnesses [who have borne testimony to the

Truth], let us strip off and throw aside every encumbrance (unnecessary weight) and that sin which so readily (deftly and cleverly) clings to and *entangles* us, and let us run with patient endurance and steady and active persistence the appointed course of the race that is set before us, looking away [from all that will distract] to Jesus, Who is the Leader and the Source of our faith [giving the first incentive for our belief] and is also its Finisher [bringing it to maturity and perfection]. He, for the joy [of obtaining the prize] that was set before Him, endured the cross, despising and ignoring the shame, and is now seated at the right hand of the throne of God.

—HEBREWS 12:1–2, AMP, EMPHASIS ADDED

There are so many Christians, including Christian leaders, who have never truly gotten free. They live their lives still controlled by the mistakes of yesterday and the fear of the past catching up with them. But Christ came to redeem us and set us free. We sometimes don't understand the cross was strong enough to handle our past and present. Imagine if we all got free—nothing would stop us!

We can only minister and declare freedom from the level we have experienced it. All through the Bible great leaders—such as Noah, Abraham, Isaac, Jacob, Moses, Samson, Esther, David, Peter, Paul, and Timothy—had to get free, and so do we. I believe we sometimes head into ministry or service for God, and the problem is we are really the ones who have to get untangled. Anything in your life that has more power over you than Jesus is your real master. In other words, it is so easy to be a slave to what should have no authority over you. This makes you dangerous to others' freedom:

They brag about themselves with empty, foolish boasting. With an appeal to twisted sexual desires, they lure back into sin those who have barely escaped from a lifestyle

of deception. They promise freedom, but they themselves are slaves of sin and corruption. For you are a slave to whatever controls you. And when people escape from the wickedness of the world by knowing our Lord and Savior Jesus Christ and then get tangled up and enslaved by sin again, they are worse off than before.
—2 Peter 2:18–20, nlt

Think about the story of Lazarus. Jesus called Lazarus out of the grave and restored him to the living. He had risen from the dead, but he still had to be unwrapped from his grave clothes. He still needed to be loosed from the wrappings around him:

The dead man came out, his hands and feet wrapped with strips of linen, and a cloth around his face. Jesus said to them, "Take off the grave clothes and let him go."
—John 11:44, niv

True freedom comes not just from resurrection, but also in the further process to freedom, which is about getting untangled from what binds us. I have learned that what you will not fight today will keep you from having authority to confront tomorrow. Our biggest hindrance is not in whom we know, where we came from, or if are we gifted enough. Rather, our greatest hindrance is not being willing to get out the mirror and say, "Woe is me!"

Ten Steps to Getting Untangled

How do you say, "Woe is me"? How do you get free from your past when it owns your present? If you will allow me, I would like to take you on a journey to understanding how this happens.

Step 1: Realize God knows your name.

God has unbelievable plans for you. Isaiah 45:3 tells us, "I'll lead you to buried treasures, secret caches of valuables—confirmations that it is, in fact, I, God, the God of Israel, who calls you by your name." Can you believe that? The Creator of the universe knows you by name!

Step 2: Realize God has been spying on you.

That's right—God has read your diary! A person's diary reveals their most private secrets. I know this from experience, as I remember the time I found my sister's diary. Let's just say it got very dangerous for me. She looked upon my felony offense as something worthy of the death penalty. I am glad I was faster than her!

But God has the keys to your diary. He knows your most intimate secrets. Psalm 139:16 says, "Like an open book, you watched me grow from conception to birth; all the stages of my life were spread out before you, the days of my life all prepared before I'd even lived one day." So there is no reason to hide anything from God.

Step 3: Realize God desires every aspect of you.

God wants all of you—not just the good stuff, but also the bad. In my first book I wrote that God is not looking for perfection but rather pursuit. It is in the pursuit of God that we realize He is very selfish with us. He wants all of our attention, just as Paul teaches: "Do you see the difference? Sacrifices offered to idols are offered to nothing, for what's the idol but a nothing? Or worse than nothing, a minus, a demon! I don't want you to become part of something that reduces you to less than yourself. And you can't have it both ways, banqueting with the Master one day and slumming with demons the next. Besides, the Master won't put up with it. He wants us—all or nothing. Do you think you can get off with anything less?" (1 Cor. 10:19–22). Did you hear that? God wants all of you!

Step 4: Realize God saw you mess up.

As a father, it has always been my goal to help my son and daughter avoid the traps that lie ahead of them. Because I am older and have been through some things, that allows me to see things they cannot. There have been times where I knew it was time to go for a walk with them and check the atmosphere of their lives.

For instance, there were times with my son, Nate, that I knew he was in a battle. I could feel there was intense warfare in his life. In fact, God even allowed Karen and me to have the same dream one night that let us know he was under attack. Soon after our dreams, we were praying together and shared our dreams we had had about Nate. Immediately we went to war. It was just a few days later that we saw our son get free of what was attacking him.

God is a good Father, and that means He has even greater insight than earthly parents do, and you must realize He was there when you messed up: "Mark well that God doesn't miss a move you make; he's aware of every step you take. The shadow of your sin will overtake you; you'll find yourself stumbling all over yourself in the dark. Death is the reward of an undisciplined life; your foolish decisions trap you in a dead end" (Prov. 5:21–23).

In fact, God knew you were heading in the wrong direction all along. That is why He gave us warnings like this:

> Be careful, or your hearts will be weighed down with dissipation, drunkenness and the anxieties of life, and that day will close on you unexpectedly like a trap. For it will come upon all those who live on the face of the whole earth. Be always on the watch, and pray that you may be able to escape all that is about to happen, and that you may be able to stand before the Son of Man.
> —Luke 21:34–36, niv

So often we forget that God has a plan to keep us from the traps of life. But Proverbs 3:26 gives us this promise: "For the Lord shall be your confidence, firm and strong, and shall keep your foot from being caught [in a trap or some hidden danger]" (AMP).

Step 5: Realize the cross is where life begins.

Isn't it amazing that a dreadful and horrible place like the cross represents life? It is a place of unbelievable suffering that brings you and me unbelievable freedom. How? By demonstrating a sacrifice was required for you and me to get free.

When you bow down at the cross, it is inevitable some blood will fall upon you. The blood of Jesus sets you free! As Jesus died on the cross, He nailed your sins to the tree:

> When you were dead in your sins and in the uncircumcision of your sinful nature, God made you alive with Christ. He forgave us all our sins, having canceled the written code, with its regulations, that was against us and that stood opposed to us; he took it away, nailing it to the cross.
>
> —COLOSSIANS 2:13–14, NIV

Now is the time to get free. That means realizing that on the cross Jesus gave you the keys to freedom. Jesus took my sin on the cross, so now I must declare He is Lord of my life. You have to confess that He is Lord too:

> Say the welcoming word to God—"Jesus is my Master"— embracing, body and soul, God's work of doing in us what he did in raising Jesus from the dead. That's it. You're not "doing" anything; you're simply calling out to God, trusting him to do it for you. That's salvation. With your whole being you embrace God setting things right, and then you say it, right out loud: "God has set everything right between him and me!"
>
> —ROMANS 10:9–10

Now is the time to run after God. No more excuses! This is how you get undone.

Step 6: Walk away from your past.

So many times we allow our past to keep us locked away in a dungeon of pain. Just as my son, Nate, had to get free, we all have to get free. And through Christ we have the ability to wave good-bye to our past:

> I do not consider, brethren, that I have captured and made it my own [yet]; but one thing I do [it is my one aspiration]: forgetting what lies behind and straining forward to what lies ahead, I press on toward the goal to win the [supreme and heavenly] prize to which God in Christ Jesus is calling us upward.
>
> —PHILIPPIANS 3:13–14, AMP

The apostle Paul was saying it is time to forget the old life—that God is calling us up and not down. Here is an acrostic I have shared for many years about this using the word *forget:*

- **F**orgive: Refuse to carry the hurt of the past into the future.
- **O**vercome: Take your rightful place as a Christian and get free.
- **R**epent: Truly walk away from the sin in your life.
- **G**row: Learn to go deep in God.
- **E**nter: God's door is open for you to come right in.
- **T**ransform: Become brand-new in Christ in your heart and mind.

No matter what has happened, God knows the end of everything, and He has crazy awesome plans for you. He has watched your every day for your entire life. He has seen your good days and bad days. He has seen when the enemy has tried to take you out, and He has plans for you regardless of what you have faced.

Step 7: Experience the power of forgiveness.

One of the major steps to freedom is when we forgive others for hurting or harming us. In fact, this is a priority on your journey to freedom. Jesus expects us to let go of our offenses: "In prayer there is a connection between what God does and what you do. You can't get forgiveness from God, for instance, without also forgiving others. If you refuse to do your part, you cut yourself off from God's part" (Matt. 6:14–15).

> The remnant chooses to let go of past hurts in order to experience the freedom that comes with forgiving and moving forward.

I'll be honest: it has taken me years to understand how to achieve this. Sure, it's easy to *say* you forgive someone, but actually *doing* it can be much harder than imagined. Forgiveness is something we all desire to receive but rarely desire to give away. This is because the pain inflicted upon us has incredible strength.

Our wounds can cause us to walk on crutches instead of soaring on wings. We get caught in the trap of reliving our hurts and offenses on a daily basis. Those memories can cause fear and pain to rise up. But forgiving others will actually allow us to begin to heal. It is time to love again.

Your freedom is tied to forgiving the person or persons who have hurt you. It isn't about them; it is about you moving forward. Forgiveness doesn't mean you invite that person to hurt you again, but it does mean you release what they did so you can no longer be wounded by it. You choose to let it go. You choose to not see the pain they caused you but rather your ability to walk away from it. You choose to allow Jesus to stand between you and that person so you see Jesus and not them.

Forgiveness is not my acceptance of another person's

actions toward me but rather my ability to release to God the offense I've been gripping in my hands in order to free my spirit to move forward. Unforgiveness is the chain that holds me to my offender. Forgiveness is the key that unlocks the chain holding me to them and allows me to escape and walk away. By forgiving, I am no longer held hostage by the pain another person attempted to place on me. God wants this for you too.

Step 8: Become a kid again.

How many times have you heard your parents say, "Would you please grow up?" You know what's crazy? God says stuff like, "Quit growing up! Be a child!" This amazes me. If you really want to see God, if you really want to be invited onto His lap, if you really want to be defended by Him, and if you really want to understand Him…then be like a child. It seems so weird! But God says He wants us to start over and grow in Him. Be a child again! This is exactly what happens when we get untangled and undone.

God loves you so much that you can literally crawl up on His lap and say, "Dad, I need to talk. I need direction. I need wisdom. I need peace." He has called you to freedom. I think so often, as believers, we think we have to make relationship happen with God. We feel if we please Him, maybe He will like us. No! It doesn't work that way. He likes what He created and stands ready to help you in all matters.

Now, get ready—these verses will rock you:

> This resurrection life you received from God is not a timid, grave-tending life. It's adventurously expectant, greeting God with a childlike "What's next, Papa?" God's Spirit touches our spirits and confirms who we really are. We know who he is, and we know who we are: Father and children. And we know we are going to get what's coming to us—an unbelievable inheritance! We go through exactly what Christ goes through. If we

go through the hard times with him, then we're certainly going to go through the good times with him!
                                    —ROMANS 8:15–17

I love when it says, "What's next, Papa?" That is a transformational thought! My little girl loves to crawl up in my lap at night. Sometimes we don't even talk. We are just there, holding each other. It is a moment of safety and peace. The whole world could crash around us, and we are just fine.

> The remnant has found freedom in the arms of a loving Savior who has not only forgiven their past but also now has authority over their future.

That is what God has called us to do—declare every morning, "What's next, Papa?" God is only as far away as a whisper from your lips or a cry from your spirit. When you become God's child, it changes everything about you. There is a confidence you can have that is so bold and refreshing. Believe it or not, you even get to stand in line for an inheritance:

> You can tell for sure that you are now fully adopted as his own children because God sent the Spirit of his Son into our lives crying out, "Papa! Father!" Doesn't that privilege of intimate conversation with God make it plain that you are not a slave, but a child? And if you are a child, you're also an heir, with complete access to the inheritance.
>   —GALATIANS 4:6–7

Step 9: Experience the gifts of the Spirit.

Now that you have encountered the beginning of freedom, you need to understand Jesus doesn't leave you as an orphan (John 14:18). In fact, the Bible is clear that you are not a slave but rather have been adopted into the family—and because you are a member of the family, God has given you weapons with which to do battle. It is impossible to go to battle and win without weapons!

We know that the weapons we fight with are not "carnal," according to 2 Corinthians 10:3–6. That means we don't fight using the weapons the world would use. Look at how *The Message* Bible puts it:

> The world is unprincipled. It's dog-eat-dog out there! The world doesn't fight fair. But we don't live or fight our battles that way—never have and never will. The tools of our trade aren't for marketing or manipulation, but they are for demolishing that entire massively corrupt culture. We use our powerful God-tools for smashing warped philosophies, tearing down barriers erected against the truth of God, fitting every loose thought and emotion and impulse into the structure of life shaped by Christ. Our tools are ready at hand for clearing the ground of every obstruction and building lives of obedience into maturity.

The weapons God gives us are His Word and His Spirit. We have the gifts of the Spirit (1 Cor. 12:1–11) for battle and the fruit of the Spirit (Gal. 5:22–23) for life. Together they are a powerful combination. God gave us His Spirit so we can stand our ground. We can do warfare in the unseen world through prayer and intercession that produce victories in the seen world.

The Holy Spirit is proof that God likes you. Did you know God will give you a new prayer language called praying in other tongues (1 Cor. 14:5, 13)? This is a language between you and God. How do you get it? Just ask! Remember, Jesus gave us a promise in Matthew 7:7–8: "Ask and it will be given to you; seek and you will find; knock and the door will be opened to you. For everyone who asks receives; he who seeks finds; and to him who knocks, the door will be opened" (NIV). I believe this gift opens the door for other gifts, like flowing in the prophetic, signs and wonders, gifts of healing, and words of knowledge. They are all different gifts, but all have the same Spirit (1 Cor. 12:4).

These gifts are given from above as an encouragement. The apostle Paul laid it out in pretty simple terms for us:

> There are different kinds of gifts, but the same Spirit. There are different kinds of service, but the same Lord. There are different kinds of working, but the same God works all of them in all men. Now to each one the manifestation of the Spirit is given for the common good. To one there is given through the Spirit the message of wisdom, to another the message of knowledge by means of the same Spirit, to another faith by the same Spirit, to another gifts of healing by that one Spirit, to another miraculous powers, to another prophecy, to another distinguishing between spirits, to another speaking in different kinds of tongues, and to still another the interpretation of tongues. All these are the work of one and the same Spirit, and he gives them to each one, just as he determines.
>
> —1 CORINTHIANS 12:4–11, NIV

Do we all have the same gifts? Not always, but the Bible says we should desire to have all of them (1 Cor. 12:31). How do you receive the gifts of the Spirit? It starts with simply inviting the Holy Spirit to do a work in your life, always being open to what God has for you. God will reveal to you the gifts in His time. For example, you might just be driving along praying when all of a sudden a new tongue comes forth. Wouldn't that be cool? It happened that way to my wife.

I recently read two quotes on Twitter from John Bevere that were taken from his new book *The Holy Spirit*. I thought they were awesome. The first tweet said, "The Holy Spirit is not a commodity to be desired; rather He is a person to be honored and invited." The second quote said, "The Holy Spirit comes within us for relationship, and upon us, baptizes us, to empower us to do what were called to do." These quotes summarize what I'm saying here. Get ready for a really fun adventure!

Step 10: Live a life of freedom.

Now that you are undone, it is time to stay free. You are forever indebted to the cross. You do not have the right to go back to the old way of life. Paul tells us:

> Since, then, we do not have the excuse of ignorance, everything—and I do mean everything—connected with that old way of life has to go. It's rotten through and through. Get rid of it! And then take on an entirely new way of life—a God-fashioned life, a life renewed from the inside and working itself into your conduct as God accurately reproduces his character in you.
>
> —EPHESIANS 4:22–24

Live your life in the presence of God, for that is where you will continually find freedom. As Psalm 16:11 says, "You will show me the path of life; in Your presence is fullness of joy, at Your right hand there are pleasures forevermore" (AMP).

You are chosen to not only get free but also stay free. At the moment you became a believer in Jesus Christ, your final destination changed. You are a temple and not a shack. The Holy Spirit lives in you! That means you are to live a life worthy of representing the Savior. You have to make up your mind that the old life represented death and your new life represents victory.

That being said, now it is time to start transforming your city. That's because you are accountable to your encounter. You must do something with the remnant mantle since you are choosing to partake of it. Spread the news about the One who can unwrap and untangle each one of us. Look what Jesus said about how to do this:

> Jesus sent his twelve harvest hands out with this charge: "Don't begin by traveling to some far-off place to convert unbelievers. And don't try to be dramatic by tackling some public enemy. Go to the lost, confused people right here in the neighborhood. Tell them that the kingdom is here. Bring health to the sick. Raise the dead. Touch the untouchables. Kick out the demons. You have been treated generously, so live generously."
>
> —MATTHEW 10:5–8

He was talking to you and me!

Now that you have chosen to get untangled, the remnant must get free. Step up and be the remnant!

Chapter 5

THEY WERE WRONG!

The remnant of Jacob will be in the midst
of many peoples like dew from the LORD,
like showers on the grass, which do not
wait for man or linger for mankind.

—MICAH 5:7, NIV

Dear Remnant,
Once you have experienced freedom,
you must stop letting the world define
you. Instead, you define the world. The
most powerful weapon the remnant has
in their arsenal is truth—not relative
truth, but the uncompromising truth laid
out in God's Word.

A S I TRAVEL this nation and world speaking to tens
of thousands of students and adults, I burn with the
desire to tell them to awaken to a new life in Christ and to
cast off the bonds society wants to place upon them. These
are those who have made it out of the "womb of life" only to
hear the voices of dissent telling them their value is less than
what God has planned for them.

I have come to tell you they are wrong! Most of this generation is so tired of being defined by the world. We are not
called to live in the constraints of what the world says but
by who the Father says we are. We are His children! It's just
like my dad once said to me: "The remnant is the group who

no longer needs to find their value from what others think of them, but they find their value in getting something from God. They, in return, give what they got from God to others to make them more valuable."

We must redefine a generation that has been under attack since conception. The apostle John said, "What marvelous love the Father has extended to us! Just look at it—we're called children of God! That's who we really are. But that's also why the world doesn't recognize us or take us seriously, because it has no idea who he is or what he's up to" (1 John 3:1).

You Have Value

Talking to you about this reminds me of the very special date that changed my family's life and teaches this exact same concept. That date was October 26, 2003, and the place was Nanchang, China. It was dusk outside. We had traveled all day to finally arrive at a place that had been a two-year journey for us. On this day we would be adopting our beautiful little girl. We could hear the noise of the children and orphanage workers milling around as we climbed the stairs in a government building. Even the smells of that night are engrained in my psyche.

As I walked with my family past a small room, I noticed one beautiful little girl sitting by herself near the back of the room. At that moment my heart leapt. I knew I had just seen my daughter for the first time. There were other babies in the room, but I knew—I just knew!

I said to Karen, "I just saw her, and she saw me! We made eye contact!"

We were ushered to another room to await our daughter being brought to us. Nate, my son, had tears in his eyes. Karen was talking nervously. It seemed like it took forever. As one family after another received their new little angel, we waited. And we kept on waiting until finally it was our turn. Would she come to us? Would she accept us? We were so nervous. But as the orphanage director, Mr. Rong, handed us our beautiful little gift, all fears left. She stared into our eyes and then wrapped her arms around her new mama's neck. She was finally safe! Finally free to grow up and have a life!

We changed her name to Abigail, which means "my father's joy." We not only changed her name but also declared her destiny.

Why do I share this? Because according to Abby's birth nation, she wasn't very valuable. In fact, China has a one-child policy that doesn't fare well for little girls. But they are wrong! You see, Abby is God's child. She is His precious little gift from heaven.

And just as Abby's life was redefined when she met her family, the only way to free an entire generation is to remind them they have a loving heavenly Father. They are not orphaned or abandoned. This generation must get past the orphan spirit that has tried to rest upon them. Jesus made us a promise in John 14:15–17: "If you love me, you will obey what I command. And I will ask the Father, and he will give you another Counselor to be with you forever—the Spirit of truth. The world cannot accept him, because it neither sees him nor knows him. But you know him, for he lives with you and will be in you" (NIV).

God loves us so much that He gave His Spirit to us. In fact, the Holy Spirit is proof that God loves hanging out with us. He enjoys being our Father and having us as His children. Look again at what it says in Romans 8:

> This resurrection life you received from God is not a timid, grave-tending life. It's adventurously expectant, greeting God with a childlike "What's next, Papa?" God's Spirit touches our spirits and confirms who we really are. We know who he is, and we know who we are: Father and children. And we know we are going to get what's coming to us—an unbelievable inheritance! We go through exactly what Christ goes through. If we

go through the hard times with him, then we're certainly going to go through the good times with him!
—ROMANS 8:15–17

God has an adventurous life for all of us. He has an inheritance saved for you! But first we have to accept the very image of God in our lives.

You Have a Name and a Face

In September 2012 I was in Manteca, California, to speak at a large youth conference called Glory Fall. Early in the day I decided to go for a jog and get some prayer time in. My heart was being stirred by the Holy Spirit for that night's service. I noticed a shiny coin lying on the ground as I was jogging. And this will prove to you that I don't jog very fast—I was excited! I thought I had found a quarter or at the least a nickel. But as I picked it up, I realized it was just a small, round, punched-out piece of metal with no value. "Ugh," I thought. "There's no value to this piece of metal. It doesn't have the face of a Founding Father on it like real money does."

Immediately I felt the Holy Spirit tell me to pick up the metal piece again. As I held it in my hand, I felt God speak to me that this coin represented a generation that needs identity. Their value will come when they have the face of the Father upon them.

I raced back to my hotel room and wrote a message about this idea, and that night we saw God transform hundreds of lives. We also saw the miraculous disappearance of scars off bodies of students who had been cutters.

For years I have heard that this is the "nameless, faceless generation." That statement has never quite settled well in my spirit. On that morning while jogging, I realized why: that statement is not correct. There is no such thing as a nameless, faceless generation. Either this generation will have the identity of God, or they will have the identity of the world. It is called face value.

Jesus became our face, according to the Book of Romans:

> For what the law was powerless to do in that it was weakened by the sinful nature, God did by sending his own Son in the likeness of sinful man to be a sin offering.
> —ROMANS 8:3, NIV

The fact is that your identity comes through Christ if you are a Christian. Jesus took our place: "How? you ask. In Christ. God put the wrong on him who never did anything wrong, so we could be put right with God" (2 Cor. 5:21).

YOU HAVE A PLACE

I am reminded of how Nathanael, a disciple of Christ, first responded to his friend Philip who had just become a follower of Christ. Philip had a desire to see his friend also follow Christ, so he started telling him about Jesus of Nazareth. Look at Nathanael's initial response: "'Nazareth! Can anything good come from there?' Nathanael asked. 'Come and see,' said Philip" (John 1:46, NIV).

As you can see, Jesus was being defined right up front by the town from which He came. Why? Because so many times value is placed not on where a person is going but on where they have been. Nazareth was not a very nice place. It was not an upscale community from which you might think a king would derive. In fact, some say it probably had a population of well under five hundred people.[1] Wow! Jesus came from a town smaller than where I was raised! I spent the last few years of high school in a place called Oneonta, Alabama, which had a population just over five thousand. I often joke that I came from a town with one red light and that Karen, my wife, came from a town in Georgia that couldn't afford a red light, so they just had a flashing sign.

This should excite everyone living in a small town because

it tells us God raises people up from places that are unfamiliar to most people. Right now he is moving on the hearts of future great leaders in small villages, tiny towns, and those from the backwoods. I love what the Bible says about who God raises up to serve Him:

> Take a good look, friends, at who you were when you got called into this life. I don't see many of "the brightest and the best" among you, not many influential, not many from high-society families. Isn't it obvious that God deliberately chose men and women that the culture overlooks and exploits and abuses, chose these "nobodies" to expose the hollow pretensions of the "somebodies"?
>
> —1 Corinthians 1:26–28

I love that verse because it flies in the face of the way most think. (And by the way, if you represent any of the descriptions above, then you're a great candidate for becoming remnant!)

But let's first look at what has already tried to define you.

Three Identity Creators

Three areas most often define a generation. They are culture, words, and experiences. I will break down each of these for you, but to be clear what I think about them, let me firmly declare, "They are wrong!"

1. Culture

The noise of the culture has reached an ear-piercing scream. I wrote a chapter about this noise of the culture in my first book, *Why Is God So Mad at Me?* There I went into detail about the attack from culture on the minds and hearts of this generation. But I feel I must go even deeper in this book.

Culture is doing its best to rewrite history, declare what it says is valuable, and get you to relinquish your right to be you. The world will do everything it possibly can to bring you down to its level. But God has called you to rise above the noise of the culture.

We will never become God's remnant if we do not understand the world in which we live. I shared the following passage in the last chapter, but I must emphasize it once again. We are in an all-out battle:

> The world is unprincipled. It's dog-eat-dog out there! The world doesn't fight fair. But we don't live or fight our battles that way—never have and never will. The tools of our trade aren't for marketing or manipulation, but they are for demolishing that entire massively corrupt culture. We use our powerful God-tools for smashing warped philosophies, tearing down barriers erected against the truth of God, fitting every loose thought and emotion and impulse into the structure of life shaped by Christ. Our tools are ready at hand for clearing the ground of every obstruction and building lives of obedience into maturity.
>
> —2 Corinthians 10:3–6

God has not only given you the gifts of the Spirit to battle, but as this passage teaches, He also has given you other "God-tools" to "demolish" that "massively corrupt culture." It is time to realize who you are. You don't have to bow down to what you have been called to overcome. We have God-tools at hand! And the greatest weapon you have is realizing you're His child.

For decades the youth of our nation have steadily headed down a path of destruction. It didn't happen overnight. The enemy has been meticulously using culture to subvert God's plan for years. One of my favorite teachers and apologists, Dr. Ravi Zacharias, describes the attack on this generation:

> In the 1950s kids lost their innocence. They were liberated from their parents by well-paying jobs, cars, and

lyrics in music that gave rise to a new term—the generation gap.

In the 1960s, kids lost their authority. It was a decade of protest—church, state, and parents were all called into question and found wanting. Their authority was rejected, yet nothing ever replaced it.

In the 1970s, kids lost their love. It was the decade of me-ism dominated by hyphenated words beginning with self. Self-image, Self-esteem, Self-assertion... It made for a lonely world. Kids learned everything there was to know about sex and forgot everything there was to know about love, and no one had the nerve to tell them there was a difference.

In the 1980s, kids lost their hope. Stripped of innocence, authority, and love and plagued by the horror of a nuclear nightmare, large and growing numbers of this generation stopped believing in the future....

In the 1990s kids lost their power to reason. Less and less were they taught the very basics of language, truth, and logic and they grew up with the irrationality of a postmodern world.

In the new millennium, kids woke up and found out that somewhere in the midst of all this change, they had lost their imagination. Violence and perversion entertained them till none could talk of killing innocents since none was innocent anymore.[2]

We must open our eyes to what is taking place in our neighborhoods, cities, and nation. David asked God in Psalm 119:18, "Open my eyes to see the wonderful truths in your instructions" (NLT). We must rise up and take a stand. The sin of the religious is to flee from responsibility. But God is calling His remnant to take a stand. Paul emphasized this when he said, "Christ has set us free to live a free life. So take your stand! Never again let anyone put a harness of slavery on you" (Gal. 5:1). One of my favorite quotes is attributed to Sir

Edmond Burke, which says, "The only thing necessary for the triumph of evil is for good men to do nothing." This could be the greatest hour of the bride of Christ—the moment where each of us realizes, again, that we are the rag in the hand of God sent to clean up the messes.

But we must stand for truth. Truth is a part of the armor of God that we are called to wear as believers. Ephesians 6:14 says, "Stand firm then, with the belt of truth buckled around your waist, with the breastplate of righteousness in place" (NIV). The apostle Paul was letting us know that we must be surrounded by truth—that truth is what will hold up the trousers of life. You will end up being a "spiritual streaker" without truth, so Paul instructs us to buckle it around us. That means lock it in place!

Truth is under attack. In fact, only 6 percent of this generation still believes in absolute moral truth.[3] Absolute moral truth is the understanding that facts do not change even when culture no longer agrees. The understanding of absolute truth has now been relegated to an op-ed column created by a reporter in which it is formatted to be just above bigotry and just below yesterday's old-fashioned morals.

At a time when reason and heart conviction only exist when they don't get in the way of desire and personal freedom, secular humanism and hedonism are now the victors of the day. What is secular humanism? "Humanism viewed as a system of values and beliefs that are opposed to the values and beliefs of traditional religions."[4] What is hedonism? An age-old philosophy that states "pleasure or happiness is the most important goal in life."[5] In very simple terms, a hedonist strives to maximize net pleasure (pleasure minus pain).

So, we have a generation who believes that God has no place in our lives or in our day-to-day plans. The secularist and even the religious have asked God to go into a closet and stay out of the way to make room for other closets to open.

The invasion of worldliness is not new, but it has become

as bold as a neon sign. I am reminded of what David F. Wells said: "Worldliness is what makes sin look normal in any age and righteousness seem odd."[6] I am convinced once we remove God from the equation of society, then we will become a nation deemed for ruin. Can we be saved? Yes, but only if the remnant of God leads the way.

> The remnant stands on truth until
> the shifting sand of compromise
> slides from underneath their feet
> to reveal the rock of salvation.

Paul said it this way: "See to it that no one carries you off as spoil or makes you yourselves captive by his so-called philosophy and intellectualism and vain deceit (idle fancies and plain nonsense), following human tradition (men's ideas of the material rather than the spiritual world), just crude notions following the rudimentary and elemental teachings of the universe and disregarding [the teachings of] Christ (the Messiah)" (Col. 2:8, AMP).

We must awaken to truth. Culture is winning! Truth is lost only when the strongest voices no longer speak or care to speak. As the remnant, we can no more ignore truth than we can get away with not telling it. It is our innate duty. If we are quiet, then the lies win.

Our inability to recognize right and wrong is due to years of ignoring the pleading of the Spirit. We also have now had years of propaganda that have dissolved our biblical stand on issues. There is a term we must all remember. Social scientists have labeled it *cognitive dissonance*. Cognitive dissonance is "a psychological conflict resulting from incongruous beliefs and attitudes held simultaneously"[7]; in other words, an uncomfortable feeling caused by holding two contradictory ideas simultaneously. The "ideas" or "cognitions" in question may include attitudes, beliefs, the awareness of one's behavior, and facts. The theory of cognitive dissonance proposes that people have a motivational drive to reduce dissonance by changing their attitudes, beliefs, and behaviors or by justifying or rationalizing their attitudes, beliefs, and behaviors.

When you know the truth and you choose to ignore it, this is called *rationalization*. This is how we alleviate the inner war! What is rationalization? It is the tendency to create additional reasons or justifications to support one's choices. This is the anxiety that comes with the possibility of having made a bad decision, so we rationalize the decision. In other words, it is the inner conflict of truth versus my behavior or perceived ideas.[8]

So, what does that mean? We tend to allow our reasoning to overwhelm the truth we know in our everyday decisions. We say things such as:

- "Did God really say that?"
- "Those were Bible days!"
- "Culture has changed, and I have to go along with the culture."
- "Everybody can't be wrong."
- "Everyone is allowed to love whomever they want."

It bleeds into our families too when we say things such as:

- "I don't want my kids or myself to be ostracized."
- "It's just for fun."
- "I'm stronger than the images on the screen."
- "We balance what we watch."
- "I can look at the menu as long as I don't order."
- "I'm just exploring my inner self."
- "We live in America—the Constitution protects me."

- "I have the right to do whatever I want."
- "My actions don't hurt anyone else."
- "I want my kids to be more popular than I was, so I'm removing the boundaries."

All of these are examples of ignoring the God voice in your life. In Christian terms, it equates to brushing off the Holy Spirit. It means ignoring what you know is right. If we ignore the Holy Spirit even though our doubts overwhelm us, then we ease our internal conflict by avoiding commitment to a particular truth. So, as Christians, we have learned to subdue the Jesus in us due to the world around us!

The writer of Hebrews gave us a stern warning: "So, as the Holy Spirit says: 'Today, if you hear his voice, do not harden your hearts as you did in the rebellion, during the time of testing in the desert'" (Heb. 3:7–8, NIV). The inner voice is the Holy Spirit calling out to you. The Bible says in Romans 8:26, "The Spirit helps us in our weakness" (NIV). Twice the apostle Paul told the Corinthians that the Spirit is a deposit guaranteeing what is to come. God is continually calling out to you. He loves you so much that He is trying to keep you from going down a path of pain. God is not anti-fun, but He is anti-pain!

The world will do everything it can to bring you down to its level. Cultural influences are constantly challenging and taunting you. Christians, according to the media and pundits, are depicted as a fascist group of disingenuous, unthinking, weak-minded zombies. They are also depicted as dumb, racist, and closed-minded. We are accused of using the "God answer" to avoid thinking. Those are just a few accusations the world loves to place on Christians.

Doesn't that just tick you off? Folks, we have not presented our case properly! Throwing a scripture out there and tucking our tails in anger will not work. Our worldviews must always be biblically based and line up with the answer to the question "What would Jesus do?"

The forces at war with the Word of God are gaining ground on the minds of a generation. Today you are deemed a hero if you come out of the closet, as gay athlete NBA player Jason Collins did in the May 6, 2013, issue of *Sports Illustrated*. You're ridiculed as a religious fanatic, however, if you drop to your knees and pray as NFL player Tim Tebow has done so many times. Perversion and sexual desire are now more accepted than a life of consecration.

I truly believe we are called to love everyone, but that does not mean we have to agree with every lifestyle. We must walk in compassion, but please don't mistake compassion as condoning behavior contrary to God's Word. Compassion is, in great measure, the love language of the cross, but convictions force each of us to stand firm on the truth.

I must warn you: when absolute moral truth is removed from a society and humanism and hedonism become the loudest voices in society, then the desire to live a godly life will become even more difficult because it means you walk with a bull's-eye on your back.

From the playground to the university campus, there is a direct attack from the enemy to remove God from our nation. The rise of atheism and agnosticism has forced us all to live on edge because our religious rights—and those of Christians in particular—are no longer considered valid. Most atheists today believe their message is their religion. They believe the Bible is just a bunch of stories and poetry but definitely not a life source. Here's what well-known atheist apologist Richard Dawkins said: "The Bible should be taught, but emphatically not as reality. It is fiction, myth, poetry, anything but reality. As such, it needs to be taught because it underlies so much of our literature and our culture."[9] Only 9 percent of American adults profess to be atheists,[10] but their voices are very loud.

What about the media? The media have done a great job convincing the world all religion is dangerous. Because of the rise of Islamic militant attacks around the globe, many now believe all religion is bad. I have often said religion is man's search for God, but once we find Him, it becomes a relationship. We do not need more religion; we do, however, need lots of relationship. Relationship is what Christianity is all about. In fact, it started with a Father sharing His Son with a world in need of a Savior, yet so many believe that religion does more harm than good.

Christianity is also so often poorly represented. In March 2012 *The American Interest* magazine posted an article called "Faith: As Not Seen on TV." Here is an excerpt from the article:

> Rather, we take exception to the fact that Christians in the media are almost uniformly shown as hypocrites, idiots, bigots and so on.... "where is the Christian love?" Contemporary television and film producers go out of their way to paint moving, sympathetic portraits of everyone from bullied gay teenagers to sex addicts and Mafia wives, but somehow run up a massive empathy deficit when it comes to men and women of faith.[11]

Many Christians believe our religious freedoms are under attack in the United States. I am reminded of the experience of sitting across the table from a man I consider a modern-day hero. His name is David Green, and he is the founder of Hobby Lobby. Hobby Lobby is a Christian-based craft and hobby company that has given hundreds of millions of dollars to missions. This billion-dollar Christian company came under attack recently by the government because of its refusal to join in the government-mandated Affordable Care Act health insurance. The reason Hobby Lobby refuses to take part is that there is a provision in the health care act that provides for abortion coverage. David Green and his company are making a stand that has cost them millions of dollars.

David is not alone. Here are some findings from the Barna Institute:

Many Americans express significant angst over the state of religious freedom in the U.S. Slightly more than half of adults say they are very (29%) or somewhat (22%) concerned that religious freedom in the U.S. will become more restricted in the next five years. As might be expected, those who are religious are more concerned than those who aren't—particularly Christians more so than those adherents to other faiths. Practicing Protestants (46% very concerned) are more worried about this prospect than others; yet, 30% of practicing Catholics are also concerned. Barna-defined evangelicals, who meet a series of nine theological criteria, are among the most likely to be concerned about such restrictions (71%).[12]

Most Christians understand that the noise of the culture is winning the war. Whether it is the IRS targeting conservative and Christian groups for scrutiny, even asking them to fill out forms sharing what they prayed about, or the constant mainstream media attacks, the war is raging. Christians realize that outside forces are doing everything they can to remove Christian values from today's culture. Again, Barna notes:

More than half of Americans (57%) believe "religious freedom has become more restricted in the U.S. because some groups have actively tried to move society away from traditional Christian values." As might be expected, this opinion is again more common among practicing Catholics (62%) and Protestants (76%) and is nearly a universal perception among evangelicals (97%).[13]

When you allow culture to declare who you are, then you have become a slave to opinion. But God has called you to be your own person. Look at what else the apostle Paul wrote in Romans:

So here's what I want you to do, God helping you: Take your everyday, ordinary life—your sleeping, eating, going-to-work, and walking-around life—and place it before God as an offering. Embracing what God does for you is the best thing you can do for him. Don't become so well-adjusted to your culture that you fit into it without even thinking. Instead, fix your attention on God. You'll be changed from the inside out. Readily recognize what he wants from you, and quickly respond to it. Unlike the culture around you, always dragging you down to its level of immaturity, God brings the best out of you, develops well-formed maturity in you.

—Romans 12:1–2

The problem is that culture has caused so many to live a life God did not plan for them. Are you buying into the lies culture espouses? Culture will tell you that you have the right to explore and do whatever you want sexually. In fact, the new term for this generation is the "Tinker Generation," because it's a generation that will try anything. But culture won't tell you the result of a life without sexual boundaries. Let me share with you some disturbing statistics concerning culture:

- Four in every five Americans started having intercourse before the age of twenty.[14]

- Many young women in this group (70 percent are age thirteen or under) stated that they had sex forced on them. By the time they are twenty, approximately 40 percent of American women have been pregnant at least once. Many of the young women in this group have little understanding of their bodies and didn't know about ways to prevent pregnancy before they began having sexual intercourse.[15]

- There are more than 19 million new cases of STDs every year in the United States.

Approximately one in two sexually active people will get one by the age of twenty-five.[16]

- More than 400,000 teen girls between the ages of fifteen and nineteen years gave birth in 2009.[17]

Culture also won't tell you the result of a life of drugs:

- An estimated 22.6 million Americans over the age of twelve were current or former illicit drug users in 2010.[18]

- The most commonly used illegal substance was marijuana. Between 2007 and 2010 marijuana usage increased to more than 17 million users.[19]

- Americans make up on only 5 percent of the world's population yet consume more than 60 percent of illegal drugs in the world.[20]

- Roughly 95 percent of addicts who don't seek help die of their addiction.[21]

- Approximately half of all state prison inmates say they were under the influence of alcohol or drugs when they committed their offense.[22]

- Roughly 25 percent of Americans die prematurely due to their addiction.[23]

- Roughly 40 percent of traffic fatalities are alcohol related.[24]

- The children of addicts and alcoholics are four times more likely to become addicts and alcoholics than children of non-addicts."[25]

Culture will also tell you marriage between a man and a woman is not important: 51 percent of the US population approves of same-sex marriage, and 43 percent say they are opposed.[26] Lastly, culture will not tell you gay marriage destroys the boundaries of civilization that have been in place since the beginning. When these boundaries are destroyed, the door is opened for any type of marriage to take place.

> The remnant walks among lost humanity
> not screaming insults or provoking
> slander, but invading with light that
> which has only known darkness.

Let's take a look at how this is playing out in our society. On June 25, 2013, the United States Supreme Court issued rulings in two highly anticipated same-sex marriage cases: *United States v. Windsor* and *Hollingsworth v. Perry*. In their rulings the court upheld states' rights to defines the boundaries of marriage, but at the same time ruled that the Defense of Marriage Act, which defines marriage between a man and woman, is unconstitutional.[27] Once again the court decided God must be confused on what He created.

I believe with all of my heart we must love and be respectful to every person, but that does not mean truth must not be shared. Truth with compassion is a powerful weapon against the lies of culture. In one swift move the Supreme Court declared that centuries of civilizations have always gotten the definition of marriage wrong. We live in a time where sexual identity controls the airwaves. Gone are the days of man plus woman equals family.

Family has been redefined by our culture to include every lifestyle. Christians are considered bigots. Gay rights activists see their work as a human rights issue. We are now living in a day where those who are not confused by their gender are at risk. In fact, on August 13, 2013, the state of California decided all children in their state will now have to share the public restrooms and locker rooms of their schools with people of the opposite sex:

California Gov. Jerry Brown signed a controversial bill into law Monday afternoon allowing the state's transgender public school students to choose which bathrooms they use and whether they participate in boy or girl sports. The law would cover the state's 6.2 million elementary and high school kids in public schools. Supporters say the law will help cut down on bullying against transgender students, The families of transgender students have been waging local battles with school districts around the country over what restrooms and locker rooms their children can use. "Now, every transgender student in California will be able to get up in the morning knowing that when they go to school as their authentic self they will have the same fair chance at success as their classmates," Masen Davis, Executive Director of Transgender Law Center, said.[28]

These are just a few examples of what culture will or will not tell you, but God has not called us to live according to culture. You are called to stand with convictions that align with God's Word. That means we must make up our mind in a perverse and confused culture to stand firm. We must declare that culture cannot have us. We belong to God!

You don't need to "sext" someone to get their attention or "twerk" with someone to make them want you. You are God's letter of life! We must be life and light to a lost and dying world. That means we must not act like the world or react like the world. That can be very tough; the battle can be very intense. But remember, we are called to be separate:

> If you belonged to the world, it would love you as its own. As it is, you do not belong to the world, but I have chosen you out of the world. That is why the world hates you.
>
> —JOHN 15:19, NIV

2. Words

If you're reading this book and can remember someone saying something to you that crushed or broke your heart, you need healing. Someone else's words have no right to define you, but so often those words do just that. Words spoken by others have a powerful ability to define each of us. So many of us have allowed words to launch or destroy our destiny. Why? Because there is power in words.

Look what the Book of Proverbs says about words: "Words kill, words give life; they're either poison or fruit—you choose." (Prov. 18:21). We love to define people by what we say they are. So often our own value is usually found in someone else's mouth. Worst yet, we take their words as truth.

It is always easy to define someone with our preconceived concepts in order to help our mind move to our next judgment. Our words can push people to a destiny that God may not have had for them. They have the power to hide away in our hearts and minds and bring undesired results.

Insecurity and fear can take root in our lives, all because of other people's words. Maybe you have been told you are dumb, ugly, fat, or even worthless. Believe it or not, I have met hundreds of people who have told me those exact words were spoken to them and that deep pain was caused in their lives as a result.

> Reckless words pierce like a sword, but the tongue of the wise brings healing.
>
> —PROVERBS 12:18, NIV

We are called to give life, and that means speaking life. We must be voices that encourage, love, and lead. We have the power to rescue people with our words.

> The words of the wicked lie in wait for blood, but the speech of the upright rescues them.
>
> —PROVERBS 12:6, NIV

The great humanitarian Mother Teresa once said, "Words which do not give the light of Christ increase the darkness."[29] The Bible warns Christians to be careful what they say: "If you claim to be religious but don't control your tongue, you are fooling yourself, and your religion is worthless" (James 1:26, NLT). We have the power to transform lives by speaking life over them.

3. Moments

Moments are the glue of our memory banks. They have the ability to bring freedom or erect prison walls. Our lives are made up of a whole bunch of moments. Some are not relevant, but many are the paths to the formation of a life. The enemy, meaning the devil, wants to monopolize your life's moments. I have actually met adults and students who have told me they have no good memories. The problem in the younger generation is that so many are being defined by bad moments or experiences. Their minds are so clouded with pain and hurt that they cannot even recall a season of happiness. This breaks the heart of God.

It is the heart of God to re-create your history by making it His story. The writer of Proverbs got it right: "Unrelenting disappointment leaves you heartsick, but a sudden good break can turn life around" (Prov. 13:12). God is the provider of the "sudden good breaks." He wants your moments back—He wants to take them and use them as your testimony. That is why Romans 8:28 promises that everything will work for the good for those who love God and have been called according to His purpose.

There are two or three moments in my life that I would define as truly dark times. Those were times it seemed I would never feel joy again. How did I make it through? I always knew Jesus was there with me. In fact, God always seems closer in dark times. There are treasures in those times. At least, that is what it says in Isaiah 45:3: "I will give you the treasures of darkness, riches stored in secret places, so that you may know that I am the LORD, the God of Israel, who summons you by name" (NIV).

We must make up our minds to turn the light on in the dark places. If God is light and in Him there is no darkness (1 John 1:5), then it is time for Him to shine. God is our nightlight in the scariness of night, and light always invades darkness.

So many have allowed dark times to define them into a shadow of what they could have become. The devil loves to declare over your life that there is no way out of your situation. When that happens, we get defined by an old moment. Our self-worth can be determined when we allow a mistake or an accident to define us. In fact, the worst kind of prejudice is not how we feel about others but how we define the one we see in the mirror!

Maybe, for example, you went on a date. The date went bad, and now you're convinced that it defined your future. Or maybe you've been told you were an accident of sexual passion gone wild. Could it be that because of the way you dressed on a certain occasion, you were suddenly labeled by others as something you're not?

Moments have the ability to defraud us all of our true identities. But defining someone—even ourselves—by one moment is to relinquish your ability to see a person's potential and thus place them in the prison of your lost expectations.

Moments of failure seem to linger way longer than moments of victory. The Bible speaks of King David's amazing victories in a short passage of 2 Samuel 8, but his failure takes up six chapters in 2 Samuel. One of the greatest human fallacies is locking people in the time warp of yesterday's failure. Grace is awesome to receive but often hard to give to others. Someone once said, "Success is not final. Failure is not final. It is the courage to continue that counts."

The Bible is full of people who could have easily been defined by their past, but God had greater plans. If many of the people in the Bible were defined by their worst moments, then think about this:

- Abraham wouldn't have had Isaac.
- Moses would have hidden forever.
- Ruth would have never remarried.
- Joseph would have died in a pit.
- David would have been left in a field to watch sheep.
- Daniel would have been eaten by the lions.
- Jonah would have been fish food.
- Peter would have died holding a rod and reel.
- Paul would still be called Saul.
- Jesus would have been aborted. (Think about that one!)

You are not defined by your moments. The enemy wants you to stop at your worst moment, caught in a life of regrets, but please don't stop where you should have died. Jesus didn't! You have the power to rewrite your history. Simply make up your mind to be like Jesus.

> The remnant doesn't stop where they should have died because they know Jesus didn't.

By the way, Jesus never promised we wouldn't face tough times. Look at what He said: "I have told you all this so that you may have peace in me. Here on earth you will have many trials and sorrows. But take heart, because I have overcome the world" (John 16:33, NLT). In other words, Jesus knew things would be really tough for us—just as they were tough for Him—but our true hope is eternity.

Your life is bigger than your moments. I love the promise of Psalm 91:14–16:

> "If you'll hold on to me for dear life," says GOD, "I'll get you out of any trouble. I'll give you the best of care if you'll only get to know and trust me. Call me and I'll answer, be at your side in bad times; I'll rescue you, then throw you a party. I'll give you a long life, give you a long drink of salvation!"

God loves to celebrate with you. He wants you to know there's a party on the other side of your pain. You are defined by your Father and not by your pain. Redefine your value—and remember that it isn't determined by your crowd, your crisis, or your cosmetics.

CHRIST'S RESPONSE

Did you know Jesus faced the pressure of culture, words, and moments too? I will prove this to you, but first look at what Hebrews 4:15–16 says:

> We don't have a priest who is out of touch with our reality. He's been through weakness and testing, experienced it all—all but the sin. So let's walk right up to him and get what he is so ready to give. Take the mercy, accept the help.

This scripture promises Jesus has faced everything we could possibly face. That lets us all know we don't suffer alone. Now let me show you all He faced without allowing those circumstances or situations to define him.

He faced insecurities.

Jesus was born as an illegitimate child. This means society shunned Him from the beginning. He wasn't from a good town. Remember what I shared with you earlier? Nathaniel said, "Can anything good come out of Nazareth?" (John 1:46,

NKJV). We know too, according the prophet Isaiah, that there wasn't anything special about Him:

> The servant grew up before God—a scrawny seedling, a scrubby plant in a parched field. There was nothing attractive about him, nothing to cause us to take a second look. He was looked down on and passed over, a man who suffered, who knew pain firsthand. One look at him and people turned away. We looked down on him, thought he was scum. But the fact is, it was *our* pains he carried—*our* disfigurements, all the things wrong with *us*.
>
> —ISAIAH 53:2–4, EMPHASIS ADDED

Jesus's earthly father, Joseph, died when Jesus was a teenager. And He was rejected by the very people He came to save.

He faced culture.

Jesus was considered a heretic. The religious leaders hated Him. Luke 16:14–15 tells us, "When the Pharisees, a money-obsessed bunch, heard him say these things, they rolled their eyes, dismissing him as hopelessly out of touch. So Jesus spoke to them: 'You are masters at making yourselves look good in front of others, but God knows what's behind the appearance. What society sees and calls monumental, God sees through and calls monstrous.'"

He faced words.

Jesus faced destructive words from everyone. First Peter 2:23–24 tells us, "They called him every name in the book and he said nothing back. He suffered in silence, content to let God set things right. He used his servant body to carry our sins to the Cross so we could be rid of sin, free to live the right way. His wounds became your healing."

How could Jesus face these things and still stand firm? Because He knew they were wrong about him.

He faced moments.

Not only did Jesus face every possible pain on the cross, but also He even faced abandonment. In His worst hour even His Father had to look away from Him:

> About the ninth hour Jesus cried out in a loud voice, *"Eloi, Eloi, lama sabachthani?"*—which means, "My God, my God, why have you forsaken me?"
>
> —MATTHEW 27:46, NIV

Can you imagine how He must have felt? The whole world had turned on Him, and because He took our place on the cross, even His Father had to look away. He hung there all alone, suspended in the air, and yet He could have climbed off the cross at any time. He didn't climb off of the cross, though, because He knew someday you would take up your cross (Luke 9:23).

How did Jesus make it and stand firm in a horrible day? He gained His strength not from culture, words, or moments but from what His Father said about Him.

WILL YOU DO AS JESUS DID?

Come with me to the day Jesus was baptized. This was the moment the world would learn His identity. Matthew 3:13–17 gives us the account:

> Jesus then appeared, arriving at the Jordan River from Galilee. He wanted John to baptize him. John objected, "I'm the one who needs to be baptized, not you!" But Jesus insisted. "Do it. God's work, putting things right all these centuries, is coming together right now in this baptism." So John did it. The moment Jesus came up out of the baptismal waters, the skies opened up and he saw God's Spirit—it looked like a dove—descending and landing on him. And along with the Spirit, a voice: "This is my Son, chosen and marked by my love, delight of my life."

Can you see Jesus as He acted out His death, burial, and resurrection? He goes down into the muddy Jordan River. He is an unknown person. He is just another Jew! But then something miraculous happens—heaven opens up as He emerges from the water, and His Father declares His identity.

What do we learn from this? That the Father has the power to free you from your drowning situation. It is the Father who restores hope to the family that seems lost. It is the Father who quiets voices of failure, despair, and fear. And Jesus understood this. He lived in anonymity. Nobody knew Him— that is, until Dad said who He was! In the water Jesus knew that when He came out—out of the very thing that could kill Him, out of the darkness of the Jordan—He would hear His Dad's voice.

The Father declares the same thing over you. We have been given this promise: "What marvelous love the Father has extended to us! Just look at it—we're called children of God! That's who we really are. But that's also why the world doesn't recognize us or take us seriously, because it has no idea who he is or what he's up to" (1 John 3:1). When you become a believer, Jesus becomes your identity. When you look in the mirror, you aren't meant to see yourself but the Jesus in you—because He lives in you.

Will you stand firm as Jesus did in the onslaught of culture, words, and moments? Take your cue from the One who stood tall, just as the true remnant does.

Chapter 6

THE MASSACRE OF THE INNOCENTS

I myself will gather the remnant of my flock out
of all the countries where I have driven them
and will bring them back to their pasture, where
they will be fruitful and increase in number.

—JEREMIAH 23:3, NIV

Dear Remnant,
It really is a miracle you're alive! Now
do something with the gift of life you've
received. Hear the screams of those
whose screams are silent. Heaven's play-
ground depends on you.

THE VERDICT IS in!"

Those were the words I heard on the radio as I was
driving down the road toward a secluded location to begin
writing this book. A jury in Philadelphia had just convicted
Dr. Kermit Gosnell of murder. Tears began to flow down my
face as I listened to the news reporter explain the heinous
crimes of this abortion doctor.

He was found guilty on three counts of infanticide.
Infanticide is the murder of a child within twenty-four
hours of its being born. These cases all occurred after failed
abortion procedures. Dr. Gosnell was also convicted of

involuntary manslaughter of a woman who had an abortion and died of an overdose.

One day after the conviction of Dr. Gosnell, the *New York Times* described the convictions:

> The case turned on whether the late-term pregnancies Dr. Gosnell terminated resulted in live births. His lawyer, Jack McMahon, argued that because Dr. Gosnell injected a drug in utero to stop the heart, the deliveries were stillbirths, and movements that witnesses testified to observing—a jerked arm, a cry, swimming motions— were mere spasms. But after deliberating 10 days, the jury found Dr. Gosnell guilty in the deaths of victims known as Baby A, Baby C and Baby D. He was found not guilty of murdering Baby E.[1]

I couldn't help but weep at the thought of an infant lying on a cold table in a dirty doctor's office, gasping for breath, reaching for comfort, and clinging to life. Is this where our nation has come? Have we now reached such a desperate place that a small child can lie on a table only to have his or her spine snapped by scissors because he or she is deemed not human? Why did it take a jury ten days to render a verdict of murder in this case?

Maybe it was because this doctor had been murdering children in the womb for years, but the difference is that those were legal abortions. So many were appalled at what this doctor in Philadelphia had done—but the fact is that every ninety-five seconds an abortion takes place at a Planned Parenthood location somewhere in the United States.[2]

Where is the outcry that Planned Parenthood performs more than 300,000 abortions a year? Who will speak out for those who lose their lives in what Psalm 139:15 calls "the secret place" (NIV)?

THE COURTS LET US DOWN

It has been forty years—exactly one generation, according to the Bible—since the *Roe v. Wade* case decided it was the law of the land to abort a child in the womb. More than 50 million babies have been killed since that landmark court case was decided. Now we live in a nation where life is not celebrated and a child is not deemed a child unless the court system says so. As one writer puts it, "We have pushed God and morality out of our schools and out of public life, and instead we have taught our young people that the slaughter of millions of babies is no big deal."[3]

> The remnant rescues the hurting
> and defends the fatherless.

I often hear news pundits, professors, and bystanders cite *Roe v. Wade* as their legal argument for abortion. But if you look at history, you will see the Supreme Court doesn't always get it right. It was the Supreme Court that ruled in 1857 that all people born of African descent were not legal citizens but rather property. In that landmark case, known as the Dred Scott Decision, the Supreme Court decided by a seven to two majority that black people were not legal persons, and it is commonly believed to be the worst decision ever made by the Supreme Court.

In a very similar decision, made just over one hundred years later, the Supreme Court decided by the same seven to two majority, that unborn people are not legal persons. They have no civil rights and no human rights and are therefore, legally, the property of the owner (the mother). While the court decided in 1857 that people of African descent had no rights, 116 years later it made the same ruling for unborn children. I believe that in this decision, just as before, our court system let us down.

The Fallout of *Roe v. Wade*

It really is a miracle that you are alive. That's right—you're a miracle. Why? Just as it was in the days of the early church, I believe we are living in one of the most perilous times in human history. Charles Dickens wrote in his famous novel *A Tale of Two Cities*, "It was the best of times, it was the worst of times." That statement could apply to today. I believe it is the best of times for Christians because God is pouring His Spirit out across the world. I also believe it is the worst of times because there is a major onslaught sent from hell to destroy this generation. We are living in a time when it is dangerous to be young.

The pulse of a society can be taken by how it treats its children, but it is impossible to take a child's pulse if it is just "a jerked arm, a cry, swimming motions—were mere spasms." I am reminded of what Margaret Sanger, founder of Planned Parenthood, once said: "The most merciful thing that the large family does to one of its infant members is to kill it."[4] Yes, she really did say that.

This is the same Planned Parenthood that President Barack Obama became the first sitting president to address during its yearly conference on April 26, 2013. In his closing remarks of affirmation for this tax-funded organization, he stated, "Thank you, Planned Parenthood. God bless you. God bless America."[5]

God bless America? Please understand that I deeply honor the office of the president, but I personally do not believe the president of the United States should ever stand before, encourage, and cheer on a group that is leading the massacre of the innocents. Do you?

Three weeks before the president addressed Planned Parenthood, a federal judge "ordered the Food and Drug Administration to make the 'morning-after' pill available without prescription to girls of all ages within one month"[6]— meaning a child can now walk into a store and buy an abortion pill but not allergy medicine. My little girl, Abby, who is ten years old, has to have note from home to go to the school office to use her asthma medicine at school, but a federal judge says she can go to any local drug store and purchase a drug to kill an unborn child. I shudder to think what the next forty years will bring us.

I shared this because this is all a part of what I call the massacre of the innocents. Whether it is a deranged gunman walking into Sandy Hook Elementary School in Newtown, Connecticut, and systematically killing twenty first-grade children and six adults on December 14, 2012, or a doctor in a neighborhood clinic performing abortions, the massacre of the innocents is very real! In fact, across the world children are under assault.

This generation is not only under attack in the womb, but also under attack in every facet of their lives. Child sex trafficking or forced labor is said by UNICEF to affect approximately 6 million across the world, and "in the US, 244,000 children and youth are said to be at risk of sexual exploitation; in addition, 38,600 runaway/throwaway children are at risk of sexual exploitation, sexual slavery or forced labor. Their vulnerability cannot be overestimated. Over 1 million children are exploited by the commercial sex trade alone each year."[7] The average age of children going into prostitution is said to be around twelve to fourteen years of age. This is according to statistics collected across the globe.

There is a child abandonment epidemic in the world. In fact, "Over 400,000,000 abandoned children live on their own on the streets of hundreds of cities around the world. These children live hand to mouth. They struggle to just survive the day."[8]

Even the children who live in homes in the United States are in danger. Child Help reports, "Children are suffering from a hidden epidemic of child abuse and neglect. Every year more than 3 million reports of child abuse are made in the United States involving nearly 6 million children (a report can include multiple children). The United States has among the worst records among industrialized nations—losing on average between four and seven children every day to child abuse and neglect."[9]

It really is a miracle many of us are here. Culture, science, government, and even many religions have gotten it wrong about the unborn child. And no doubt many of the remnant God planned to use were destroyed by a lie from the enemy before they were even able to experience life outside the womb.

Jesus Loves His Kids

To really know the heart of God toward His children, all you have to do is read the account of Jesus and His handlers. Jesus is out doing ministry, and those pesky kids were trying to get to Him. The disciples were playing crowd control and holding the children back. But Jesus removed the "red velvet rope" that was keeping them out. Matthew 19:14 says, "But Jesus intervened: 'Let the children alone, don't prevent them from coming to me. God's kingdom is made up of people like these.'"

Jesus loves His children! And maybe that is why the enemy does his best to destroy this generation. If Jesus loves the children, then the devil hates them. He also knows that every time God wants to change a generation, somebody gives birth.

Look at the biblical history on this. The two times when deliverers were born—Moses and Jesus—they were both targets of government at the time of their birth. For Moses, it was a decree by Pharaoh that all male babies be thrown into the Nile River (Exod. 1:22). The same thing happened when Jesus was a baby. When King Herod heard from the magi a new king had been born, he was so worried another king would take his throne that he ordered the massacre of all young boys under the age of two (Matt. 2:16). So many babies were killed that this is known as the true "massacre of the innocents."

Could we be living once again in a time we could call a massacre of the innocents? I believe we are.

GETTING THE FACTS STRAIGHT

I've shared with you a lot of statistics about the onslaught against children in this generation, and proponents of abortion have their own way of dealing with the facts. Here are some facts, though, you will never see in a Planned Parenthood brochure, all proving a child is a child at the moment of conception:

- The heart starts beating around twenty-one days.
- Electrical brain waves have been detected at six weeks. (And I ask you: If death is indicated by the absence of a brain wave, why don't pro-abortionists accept that the presence of a brain wave is a confirmation of life?)
- During the second month of pregnancy the brain and all body systems develop and are functioning a month later.
- During month three the baby sleeps, awakens, and exercises, sometimes even getting the hiccups.
- By the end of the third month the baby's own unique fingerprints are evident, as well as the sex of the baby.
- At eleven to twelve weeks the baby is sensitive to heat, touch, light, and noise. Weighing about a half pound and being about eight to ten inches long, all body systems are working.[10]

I can also promise you will never find this scripture framed and hanging on the walls of an abortion clinic:

Oh yes, you shaped me first inside, then out; you formed me in my mother's womb. I thank you, High God— you're breathtaking! Body and soul, I am marvelously made! I worship in adoration—what a creation! You know me inside and out, you know every bone in my

> body; you know exactly how I was made, bit by bit, how I
> was sculpted from nothing into something. Like an open
> book, you watched me grow from conception to birth;
> all the stages of my life were spread out before you, the
> days of my life all prepared before I'd even lived one day.
>
> —Psalm 139:13–16

All of this reminds me of a paper my son, Nate, wrote as an assignment for his eighth grade class in which it was his job to defend the rights of the unborn. Needless to say, I was very proud of the words he penned. In fact, Nate's paper has hung in a frame on the wall of my office for years, even up to the writing of this book.

Here are the contents of the eighth-grade paper in its entirety—and I say "in its entirety" because I want you to notice the remark his teacher wrote at the end of the paper:

Abortion

What would you say if you knew hundreds of babies were killed each day in the world? I'm writing about abortion. I'm definitely not for this topic. I'm writing about how it's demolishing the human race, and how these babies are really alive. I'm also writing how the babies we're killing could be the incredible ones tomorrow.

As stated previously, if we continue like this, we will just be considered another barbaric nation. These babies are not like your pet dog being put to rest. Babies have a spirit, and a dog doesn't. The law and the Bible say, "do not murder." Our nation was founded on the Bible and the law, but I think everyone has forgotten. I don't understand the people who think abortion is okay.

As mentioned above, this topic endangers the population of the world, and we are just going to let the human race go to waste. A very large portion of the mothers who abort are teenagers that aren't responsible enough to handle the consequences of their own actions. People need to start thinking about the babies and not themselves. These people need to be sentenced with murder. It may be a mother's choice, but not a mother's right.

On the whole, the babies we're killing may be the next presidents. What if this person would have established world peace? Maybe they would have found a cure for AIDS. Not only that, but that person probably would have had a family of their own. You are also killing their family.

In conclusion, abortion is killing the human race, and these babies are really alive. The people we're killing could be the next heroes. People think it's a woman's choice—that the babies aren't really alive because they are so innocent. When was the last time you heard of killing someone being okay?

Nate Schatzline
Hewitt-Trussville Middle School
8th Grade
14 years old

His teacher left a note at the bottom of the assignment, which said:

> What if Mary had aborted Jesus because she wasn't married when he was conceived? Something to think about! Good paper! (100% grade)

As I mentioned to you previously, Nate is now a youth pastor in Dallas, Texas, at Trinity Church. I guess even at a young age he understood the battle over a generation and that he must be remnant!

Not only does this paper declare truth, but also I am really proud of Nate's public school teacher, who added the note at the bottom. She represents the remnant spirit too, and I pray more teachers will throw off political correctness and realize that their simple notes at the end of a student essay can add a voice of authority to this generation.

How Does a Remnant Respond?

Why would I share all of this, and what does this have to do with being remnant? Because of all that's happening, I can't help but believe we're on the verge of seeing deliverers rise up in a generation. Why else would the enemy work so hard to destroy them? That is why the remnant must rise!

Remember that one of the definitions of remnant is "what is left over." For years we have watched a generation rise up that battles deep anger, abandonment, hurt, and fear. I have personally seen tens of thousands of young people flood altars looking for answers, whether it's about their parents' divorce, abuse they face at home, or simply trying to understand why life is so hard.

I am convinced we are ripe for the greatest outpouring of God's Spirit in history because mourning is always the precursor to prophetic moves of God. This generation has faced more pain and rejection than all previous generations. This generation is looking for power with love, joy with relationship, and freedom from pain. This generation desires a mandate from above. They want to be challenged to go deep in God. They are not ashamed of the supernatural.

If the church understood the boldness and passion of this generation, I believe we would release a whole surge of young people to lead a revolution for God. There are so many powerful youth and adult movements taking place across the globe. Maybe it is because we are now entering into the fulfillment of Joel 2:28 and the promise of Acts 2:17: "And afterward, I will pour out my Spirit on all people. Your sons and daughters will prophesy, your old men will dream dreams, your young men will see visions" (Joel 2:28, NIV). I honestly believe the enemy is doing everything he can to stop a generation from living.

Perhaps the church needs to be reminded that Jesus was

very clear about how to build the kingdom of God. Do you remember? He said it would happen through children:

> People brought babies to Jesus, hoping he might touch them. When the disciples saw it, they shooed them off. Jesus called them back. "Let these children alone. Don't get between them and me. These children are the kingdom's pride and joy. Mark this: Unless you accept God's kingdom in the simplicity of a child, you'll never get in."
> —LUKE 18:15–17

God is about to bring forth amazing movements of power, but the enemy would love to tell us that the "movements that witnesses testified to observing—a jerked arm, a cry, swimming motions—were mere spasms."[11] This generation of remnants must push past the noise of the crowd and the lethargy of the religious and crawl into the lap of a loving Savior.

It is time for the remnant to rise up and stand for the innocent. The weeping prophet Jeremiah, who wrote the book of Lamentations, said it best: "Arise, cry out in the night, as the watches of the night begin; pour out your heart like water in the presence of the Lord. Lift up your hands to him for the lives of your children, who faint from hunger at the head of every street" (Lam. 2:19, NIV). Someone must arise and cry out! Will it be you?

Last but not least important, we must help heal the hearts of all of those who have had or been a part of an abortion. There are two victims in abortion—one is dead and one is damaged. Abortion touches all age groups of women: "It is estimated that, as of 2008, about 28% of U.S. women ages 15-64 have had abortions."[12] According to the National Abortion Federation, about 19 percent of abortions are obtained by women between the ages of fifteen and nineteen, with 33 percent obtained by women between the ages of twenty and twenty-four. Women over the age of thirty obtain about 25 percent of abortions.[13] The reason I share that is because we so often think abortion is only about teenagers and young adults, when one-fourth are over the age of thirty. "Of all U.S. women getting abortions, about 54 percent are doing so for the first time, while one-fifth have had at least two previous abortions. Of those over 20, the majority have attended college. Almost a third have been married at some point. About 60 percent have at least one child; one-third have two or more."[14]

A 2004 study by the Guttmacher Institute reported that women listed the following reasons for choosing to have an abortion:[15]

- 74 percent: "Having a baby would dramatically change my life"
- 73 percent: "Cannot afford a baby now"
- 48 percent: "Do not want to be a single mother or having relationship problems"
- 38 percent: "Have completed my childbearing"
- 32 percent: "Not ready for (another) child"
- 25 percent: "Do not want people to know I had sex or got pregnant"
- 22 percent: "Do not feel mature enough to raise (another) child"
- 14 percent: "Husband or partner wants me to have an abortion"
- 13 percent: "Possible problems affecting the health of the fetus"
- 12 percent: "Concerns about my health"
- 6 percent: "Parents want me to have an abortion"
- 1 percent: "Was a victim of rape"
- Less than 0.5 percent: "Became pregnant as a result of incest"

We often think the unsaved are the ones who have abortions, but here is proof we are wrong: "Women identifying themselves as Protestants obtain 43% of all abortions in the U.S.; Catholic women account for 27%, Jewish women account for 1.3%, and women with no religious affiliation obtain 23.7% of all abortions. 18% of all abortions are performed on women who identify themselves as born-again or Evangelical."[16] That last statistic is the one that we must remember. If 18 percent of women who have had abortions are born-again evangelicals, then our churches must be places of truth and healing.

If these statistics show us anything, it is that we must realize that all around us—in our workplaces, neighborhoods, and churches—women are deeply wounded by abortion. We must be ready to show love and grace. The silent scream in our nation is the wounded hearts of those who have experienced loss of life within their wombs. Whether they were a victim of rape or incest, whether they feel they had no choice but to end the life that was created by evil violence, or whether they simply didn't want the child at that point in their life, the unborn child is not the only victim. We must be there to heal these mothers and fathers who have walked through this devastation. God has plans for them, and each one of them is a victim of culture or lies. God can use their testimony to keep others from walking down this path. That is why we have in the Bible what I call its "on purpose promise": what we have been through, God can use for His glory.

> And we know that in all things God works for the good
> of those who love him, who have been called according
> to his purpose.
>
> —ROMANS 8:28, NIV

We must wrap our arms around these individuals and show them a path to the Father's undying love and freedom. We know sin loves to deceive us and make us think a certain path is right when it is really wrong (Prov. 14:12). Those affected by abortion must be told that all of us have sinned and fallen short of the glory of God (Rom. 3:23). Most of all, we must offer grace! Jesus took our sin so we could walk in freedom.

No matter what mistakes we make, God can make us brand new (2 Cor. 5:17), and condemnation from the past loses its voice when you become God's child (Rom. 8:1). Every person who chooses Christ and declares His Lordship over their life (Rom. 10:9) is promised an eternity in heaven. That means their first stop in heaven will be at the most amazing playground, where they will get to have fun with their child who awaits.

If we want to see the remnant rise up and lead, we must understand that this remnant will have scars from decisions of the past and an awesome authority to help heal others in their future. Psalm 103:6–14 says:

> God makes everything come out right; he puts victims back on their feet. He showed Moses how he went about his work, opened up his plans to all Israel. God is sheer mercy and grace; not easily angered, he's rich in love. He doesn't endlessly nag and scold, nor hold grudges forever. He doesn't treat us as our sins deserve, nor pay us back in full for our wrongs. As high as heaven is over the earth, so strong is his love to those who fear him. And as far as sunrise is from sunset, he has separated us from our sins. As parents feel for their children, God feels for those who fear him. He knows us inside and out, keeps in mind that we're made of mud.

Will You Use Your Voice?

Late in the evening of November 4, 2012, I was sitting on a flight on my last leg of a journey home. Many on the flight were talking about the presidential election that would take place in just two days, and a lady sitting next to me began to engage me in conversation. I told her I was a minister and was traveling home from speaking at a youth conference in

New Jersey. She said, "Well, I guess I know what side of the aisle you are on concerning the presidential election."

I smiled and said, "I simply vote the Bible." I explained that Jesus was not a donkey (Democrat) or an elephant (Republican), but that He rode those things.

She laughed. Then she informed me that she had been with Planned Parenthood since the 1970s. I gathered myself emotionally, because I knew that the subsequent conversation could go downhill fast from there. But we both agreed to have a civil conversation and approach each other with friendship.

She shared about women's rights and that she believed a woman's body is hers to do with as she wishes—and she was astonished at my rebuttal as I told her I agreed with her. I said, "I do believe that each one of us owns our own bodies and must give an account for what we do while in the body."

But the next course of the conversation did not sit well with her. I said, "I own my house that I live in. I have the right to do anything I want to my house." She listened intently to see where I was going. I went on, "Since I own my house, I can even burn it down if I want—but of course I would have to pay the bank what I owe them."

She laughed, and I continued. "It is not a crime unless there is someone in my house when I burn it down. Then it is murder."

The woman looked at me intently and then said, "That is a great argument, but a woman's body is not a house."

The conversation ended, and eventually the plane landed. As the woman was getting off the plane, she turned to me and shook my hand. "Just want you to know I really enjoyed our conversation," she said. "And by the way, my guy will win on Tuesday." Her guy was, of course, President Obama.

I replied, "Then he will be my president as well for four more years!"

Fast-forward about eight months, on a Sunday night in July 2013, and you would find me just wrapping up the fourth service of the day at one of the most powerful churches I have ever had the honor of ministering at, called the Rock Family Church in Huntsville, Alabama. That evening I shared in my message this story about the conversation I had with the woman on the plane and how God had nudged me to use the analogy of owning a house when discussing abortion.

As I stood in the sanctuary talking with different people after the service, a precious lady came up to me. She grabbed my hand and, with tears flowing down her face, began to share. She was a professor of music at one of the oldest and most prestigious black universities in the South. When she had heard my analogy concerning abortion that evening, the Holy Spirit convicted her to change her ideology concerning the life of an unborn child.

She said, "I sat through the rest of your message weeping because I had been wrong for so many years. Now I must use the position that God has entrusted me with to lead young college-age ladies down the right path!"

I hugged her and told her this was her moment to make a stand for life. She now represents the remnant calling, and only eternity will tell how many lives are saved by the influence of this great leader. She has become a voice of awakening to the truth concerning the unborn. I was so proud of her stand! I know it will not be easy since she works in an academic environment that rejects, on almost all levels, the pro-life stance, but with God's help she will be a voice of reason.

Will you also use your voice?

SECTION II

THE REMNANT MUST GET REAL

Chapter 7

THE SIMEON CRY

A remnant will return, a remnant of
Jacob will return to the Mighty God.
—ISAIAH 10:21, NIV

Dear Remnant,
  Are you desperate to reveal God's
answer to the world? You were created
to declare God's glory. If you accept the
call to be the remnant, you must possess
the spirit of Simeon.

I HAVE A WHOLE list of people I want to meet when I get
to heaven. First, I want to run and fall at the feet of Jesus,
my Savior and King, and worship Him alongside my sister
and grandparents. That will be an awesome reunion! Then
there are key individuals from the Bible I want to schedule
a sit-down with—maybe even go to a coffee shop with them
(because I do believe there will be coffee in heaven!). I want
to sit down with David and the apostle John to talk about the
heart of worship. I want to meet Abraham and Moses and
talk to them about being a friend of God. I want to meet Jeremiah and Simon Peter and talk with them about brokenness.

But there is one other guy I really want to meet, and that
is a man named Simeon—a man who holds a very special
place in the birth story of Christ.

A Man With a Promise

One of the best-known passages of scriptures in the Bible is found in Luke 2. The first twenty-one verses are perhaps the most famous—we hear them read or recited at Christmas cantatas every year, and they tell the story of the actual birth of Christ. But have you ever read the rest of the chapter?

In verse 22 we learn it came time for Jesus to be presented at the temple by His parents. All firstborn males were required by law to be presented at the temple forty days after their birth. And that's where we learn about this very old man named Simeon.

The Bible says he had prayed a special prayer that he would not depart the earth without seeing God's glory. He wanted to see the fulfillment of Isaiah's prophecy that a Messiah would be born, and the Scriptures tell us the Holy Spirit had promised that he would.

According to the tradition of the Orthodox Church, this happened when he "was translating a book of the Prophet Isaiah and read the words, 'Behold, a virgin shall conceive in the womb, and shall bring forth a Son' (Is. 7:14). He thought that 'virgin' was inaccurate, and he wanted to correct the text to read 'woman.' At that moment an angel appeared to him and held back his hand saying, 'You shall see these words fulfilled. You shall not die until you behold Christ the Lord born of a pure and spotless Virgin.'"[1]

Isaiah further prophesies:

> For a child has been born—for us! The gift of a son—for us! He'll take over the running of the world. His names will be: Amazing Counselor, Strong God, Eternal Father, Prince of Wholeness. His ruling authority will grow, and there'll be no limits to the wholeness he brings. He'll rule from the historic David throne over that promised kingdom. He'll put that kingdom on a firm footing and keep it going with fair dealing and

right living, beginning now and lasting always. The zeal of GOD-of-the-Angel-Armies will do all this.

—ISAIAH 9:6–7

This prophecy, of course, speaks of Jesus, and Simeon came to believe the prophecies about the Christ would be fulfilled in his lifetime, given the encounter he had with the Holy Spirit. Besides, times were tough. People were desperate much like today. It was time for a rescuer to come on the scene.

Here is the recorded account in the Book of Luke about the day Simeon had his prayers answered:

> It had been revealed to him by the Holy Spirit that he would not die before he had seen the Lord's Christ. Moved by the Spirit, he went into the temple courts. When the parents brought in the child Jesus to do for him what the custom of the Law required, Simeon took him in his arms and praised God, saying: "Sovereign Lord, as you have promised, you now dismiss your servant in peace. For my eyes have seen your salvation, which you have prepared in the sight of all people, a light for revelation to the Gentiles and for glory to your people Israel." The child's father and mother marveled at what was said about him. Then Simeon blessed them and said to Mary, his mother: "This child is destined to cause the falling and rising of many in Israel, and to be a sign that will be spoken against, so that the thoughts of many hearts will be revealed. And a sword will pierce your own soul too."
>
> —LUKE 2:26–35, NIV

A REMNANT LIFE REVEALED

Simeon is what I call remnant. This simple man of God understood what it meant to put it all on the line for God. He made it his life's goal to see the glory. He waited! He believed! He refused to miss his moment!

Can you imagine? He had a visitation from the Holy

Spirit promising that he would encounter the Savior of the world. As he was getting ready to go to the temple that day, I imagine his body was screaming his age—many scholars believe Simeon was over two hundred years old. So he was moving much slower than he used to.

I wonder if he prayed in his morning prayers, "Lord, please let this be the day the prophecy is fulfilled." As he made his way to the temple, he no doubt passed many with whom he had walked through life's agonies and victories. Can you see it? Perhaps they waved at him and he smiled back at them with a loving, pastoral grin. Inside, his heart no doubt was racing. His spirit was longing for something more.

Then, as the people came into the temple and the families approached the priest to present their children for dedication, I imagine Simeon felt a trembling come over his body—an exhilaration of the presence he had felt the day the Holy Spirit visited him. Perhaps he looked up from his scrolls to see a young couple standing off to the side, waiting their turn. Perhaps he made eye contact with Mary and Joseph and they smiled at him with sheepish grins, for they knew whom they held in their arms.

Can you see it? Simeon strides toward them, bypassing the other families, his heart racing like never before. He says to them, "I have heard your story. I have heard the gossip. And yet you have remained faithful. May I hold your child?"

Can you see it? Mary hands the baby Jesus to the old pastor, and his tears begin to flow. As Simeon moves the blanket away from the face of the child, he begins to weep. Without a second thought for his reputation and without fear of retribution from the religious leaders there, he makes a stunning announcement. He declares as loud as possible, "Lord, I can now die. I have found all of mankind's salvation. He will be the light and glory to the world!"

That is what I call the "Simeon cry"—a cry that says, "God, please don't let me depart until I see the glory of Israel!"

Simeon could now walk into heaven a free man, free of the fear of missing out on what God was doing. It didn't matter that culture would mock him. It didn't matter that the religious world would mark him as a crazy dreamer. This man had an encounter with God, and during that encounter God told him he would see the promise. That, my friend, is the Simeon cry: "God, please don't let me die until I see Your glory!"

STANDING STRONG IN THE STRUGGLE

My wife, Karen, often shares about the stages of metamorphosis that must take place for a butterfly to grow from larva to a beautiful flying creature. What most do not realize is that it is during the time of struggle in the cocoon that the butterfly gains the strength to fly. In the same way, the remnant must understand that strength is birthed in the struggle. I don't often grow in good times, but in the rough times I have gained character and the passion to keep going.

We must make up our mind to pursue God regardless of circumstances. Trust me—I know how difficult it is. There are days in ministry and life where the only thing you can muster in your spirit to say is simply, "I am still here!" But I have felt the heartbeat of Simeon for many years. I have wanted to be one who looks past every obstacle, around every corner, and into every crevice to find my God. I want it so I can clearly declare His glory and freedom. I love the cry of Psalm 73:25–28:

> You're all I want in heaven! You're all I want on earth! When my skin sags and my bones get brittle, GOD is rock-firm and faithful. Look! Those who left you are falling apart! Deserters, they'll never be heard from again. But I'm in the very presence of GOD—oh, how refreshing it is! I've made Lord GOD my home. GOD, I'm telling the world what you do!

What is the Simeon cry? It is a personal cry that eventually becomes a public proclamation of Jesus. It is the cry from your inner spirit to see God's glory. It is ignoring the noise of the culture, moving past our personal fears, and becoming resolute that the greatest joy in life is the presence of God.

I love the heart of Simeon. He never wavered from his passion. When others probably told him to preach on popular social issues, he refused. When others advised he focus on the government and politics, he refused. Then, when time seemed to be slipping away, he had an encounter with God. He was moved by the Spirit. Luke 2:27 says, "Moved by the Spirit, he went into the temple courts" (NIV).

> The remnant cannot be defined by man's concepts because they find their value in the eyes of a Savior.

I imagine Simeon wasn't moved by what others wanted. He was different! He wasn't like what I call "those":

- Those who are satisfied with a little religion to get you by
- Those who have grown comfortable with the idea that God is just an idol to be worshipped on a weekly basis
- Those who are not willing to give their last breath for an encounter
- Those who bristle at the thought of being ostracized for truth
- Those who dream small and obtain easy dreams that consist of an office, a paycheck, and a ministry title
- Those who always look over their shoulder to see if they missed their calling

- Those who immediately react with a fear of losing themselves at the thought of being transformed by His presence
- Those who are content with experiencing God through others' eyes
- Those who think ministry is the end result of their network
- Those who think self-denial only has to do with counting calories and fat content
- Those who think the enlightening of a generation happens through stage lights and mediocre messages
- Those who keep a personal checklist that does not include a visitation of God's glory but a visitation of the flesh-eating bacteria called Self

Simeon recognized his moment had arrived. But I must warn you—it is easy to miss your moment. When God shows up, it isn't about you but about God being on display for the lost, hurting, and broken. Look what Psalm 115:1–2 says:

> Not for our sake, GOD, no, not for our sake, but for your name's sake, show your glory. Do it on account of your merciful love, do it on account of your faithful ways. Do it so none of the nations can say, "Where now, oh where is their God?"

We must guard against getting weighed down with what doesn't matter. Don't let the enemy distract you. Stay focused on your mission. God is never far away from His remnant; in fact, God is just around the corner!

> Friends, when life gets really difficult, don't jump to the conclusion that God isn't on the job. Instead, be glad that you are in the very thick of what Christ

experienced. This is a spiritual refining process, with glory just around the corner.

—1 Peter 4:12–13

Why Did God Use Simeon?

Six Ps guided Simeon's life that made him a man God used:

Prayer: He understood his prayer life was where the answers to his dreams could be found. He sought the heart of God and, in doing so, received his promise.

Purity: Simeon was a devout man. He recognized what it meant to be called and set apart by God. He refused to be religious, but rather he walked in relationship with God.

(continued on next page)

Simeon stayed focused. He didn't worry about being ostracized. He made up his mind that when God was done with him, he was ready to get out of the way. In fact, I imagine he didn't live much longer after he met the Christ because he had experienced holding the Savior in his hands. He died full! God must have been smiling at this.

Four Steps to Becoming a Modern-Day Simeon

Do you want to be a modern-day Simeon? Do you want to know what it takes? Here are four keys to getting there.

1. Run to the One who has run ahead of us.

You will either run away from God or toward Him. There is no middle ground. And when we choose to run toward God, it transforms everything about us. Hebrews 6:18–20 says, "We who have run for our very lives to God have every reason to grab the promised hope with both hands and never let go. It's an unbreakable spiritual lifeline, reaching past all appearances right to the very presence of God where Jesus, running on ahead of us, has taken up his permanent post as high priest for us, in the order of Melchizedek."

Jesus has already run our race for us. He is waiting on

you to catch up! He is our coach who's calling out, "Finish the race!"

2. Realize the transformational presence of God.

Those of us who have had encounters with God understand that something transforms inside us when we spend time with Him. Look what the apostle Paul said in 2 Corinthians 3:16–18:

> Whenever, though, they turn to face God as Moses did, God removes the veil and there they are—face-to-face! They suddenly recognize that God is a living, personal presence, not a piece of chiseled stone. And when God is personally present, a living Spirit, that old, constricting legislation is recognized as obsolete. We're free of it! All of us! Nothing between us and God, our faces shining with the brightness of his face. And so we are transfigured much like the Messiah, our lives gradually becoming brighter and more beautiful as God enters our lives and we become like him.

Purpose: Simeon knew God had a plan—that God wasn't finished with him yet. As long as there was breath in him, Simeon held out hope of seeing God's glory revealed.

Perseverance: This man refused to give up. He understood his only hope was seeing the Savior. He waited until the revelation revealed itself. He let God be God!

Passion: Simeon was zealous. He wasn't swayed by opinion, platform, or titles but only by the word of God spoken directly to him.

Proclamation: Simeon was willing to shout the truth in public. He waited for the moment when the world would listen, and then he declared that truth.

These six Ps have the power to transform culture. If you uphold them in your life, God can place the Simeon cry within your spirit too.

3. Know you are God's walking billboard.

I love what my dear friend, prophet Luke Holter, said to me in a recent phone conversation. He said, "We are mobile Upper Rooms!" We are called to be walking billboards of God's power.

You represent to the world that God can transform lives. Because of this, you are a walking billboard of transformation. You represent a life that has experienced the freedom of the cross.

> You yourselves are a case study of what he does. At one time you all had your backs turned to God, thinking rebellious thoughts of him, giving him trouble every chance you got. But now, by giving himself completely at the Cross, actually dying for you, Christ brought you over to God's side and put your lives together, whole and holy in his presence. You don't walk away from a gift like that! You stay grounded and steady in that bond of trust, constantly tuned in to the Message, careful not to be distracted or diverted. There is no other Message—just this one. Every creature under heaven gets this same Message. I, Paul, am a messenger of this Message.
>
> —Colossians 1:21–23

4. Tell the truth, no matter what.

If you want to become a modern-day Simeon, you must be prepared for the world not to understand your life's mandate. But in a world where most people are afraid to declare the truth because it will cost them preeminence and prominence, the voice of truth must scream louder. It's as Jesus said:

> Count yourself blessed every time someone cuts you down or throws you out, every time someone smears or blackens your name to discredit me. What it means is that the truth is too close for comfort and that that

person is uncomfortable. You can be glad when that happens—skip like a lamb, if you like!—for even though they don't like it, I do...and all heaven applauds. And know that you are in good company; my preachers and witnesses have always been treated like this.

—LUKE 6:22–23

I have Simeon's cry in my spirit, and I believe there are multiple millions who have that same cry. It is a cry that says, "God, please don't let me depart until I see Your glory poured out on a generation!"

Are you willing to be that type of remnant? Is there a cry in your spirit? Is it the Simeon cry?

Chapter 8

WEEPING LIONS AND ROARING LAMBS

But I will leave within you the meek and humble
[the remnant], who trust in the name of the LORD.
—ZEPHANIAH 3:12, NIV

Dear Remnant,
Your brokenness before the Savior will
determine your influence to the world
and your effectiveness in the church. The
world is not in need of a superstar, but
rather a rag in the hand of God to clean
up the mess.

IWILL NEVER FORGET the morning God spoke to me
the title of this chapter. I was at Fresh Start Church, in
Phoenix, Arizona, speaking during their annual men's conference. It was still very early in the worship service, and I
felt compelled to lie down on the floor and seek God's face
during the intimate part of the song service. As I lay on the
floor listening to the men of the house worshipping God in
a real and intimate way, I heard the voice of God say to me,
"Pat, I am looking for weeping lions and roaring lambs!"

I began trying to determine if what I had heard was real
or not. God often interjects a fresh word from heaven when
I am still before Him, but the problem is that I very rarely

actually enter into that place of rest. My schedule—and most of all my mind—never seem to stop racing.

But at the same moment I heard the Lord speak to me, my dear friend, pastor Paul Owens, stepped up to the microphone and said, "I hear a holy roar of a lion over this house for men to rise up and lead."

In that moment I knew God had spoken clearly through Paul to me.

I asked the Lord what the message meant, but He didn't answer until two weeks later. I was traveling in Singapore when it happened, and on that particular day I had gone for an early morning jog. Once again I heard the Lord say, "Pat, I am looking for weeping lions and roaring lambs."

I stopped in my tracks and said, "OK, God, what does that mean?"

> The remnant is satisfied at all times because they hunger and thirst after righteousness—and they shall be filled.

He said, "Son, for too long the lions of the kingdom of God have roared and ignored the sounds of the weeping lambs. If the lions will weep again, then the lambs will rise up with a roar."

WEEPING LIONS

My favorite animal at the zoo has always been the lion. I love to watch it, as it seems to sit without a care in the world, always aware of its surroundings yet not moved by any distractions. I have tried on many occasions to get the lion's attention, but I always failed. The confidence of a lion is surely something to be admired.

The lion has always been known as the king of the jungle. It is the fiercest of all animals, and its roar can send a chill down the back of an attacker. And as we will learn in this chapter, the lion has much to teach us about becoming remnant—and it starts with our moving toward becoming lions that weep.

Climb down from Pride Rock.

Do you remember the movie *The Lion King*? It's the first movie I took my son to see when he was just three years old. Who can forget Mufasa, the head of the lion tribe, the protector of the pride, as he stood holding his son, the lion cub Simba, in the air on Pride Rock? The animals bowed and the music blared in triumph the song "The Circle of Life." Remember that moment? Can you see it in your mind?

That's the same idea God was speaking to me about—except in reverse. For so long the Mufasas of God's kingdom have stood on "Pride Rock" while everyone around them bows. We have protected our pride for far too long. And yet the more we allow pride to lead our lives, the more we lose our influence. Proverbs 11:2 says, "When pride comes, then comes disgrace, but with humility comes wisdom" (NIV).

Pride has the ability to cause even the most influential and the most effective to fall swiftly, yet when we embrace humility, God allows us to stand tall with perseverance even in the toughest places. This is because we will have embraced our humanity and placed our trust in His divinity.

When we become the protectors of the pride, we are no longer effective Christians. Psalm 10:4 states, "In his pride the wicked does not seek him; in all his thoughts there is no room for God" (NIV). As Harold Vaughan, the founder of Christ Life Mission, has written, "Humility is the foundation of all virtue, but pride is the essence of all sin. The world system operates on the basis of pride, for all that is in the world is lust and pride (1 John 2:16). Pride and lust are root sins from which all other sins spring. Pride is the mother of evil."[1]

When we lose our pride, the lion can learn how to weep again. And we must do this, for the Bible tells us God hates pride. Proverbs 8:13 declares, "To fear the LORD is to hate evil; I hate pride and arrogance, evil behavior and perverse speech" (NIV). When we lose our fear of the Lord, we then open the door for pride to take over and wisdom to leave. But we must never forget that the "fear of the LORD is the beginning of wisdom" (Prov. 9:10, NIV). We must climb down from Pride Rock and minister in the jungle of life.

Worship the Lion of Judah.

Why is Jesus called the Lion of the tribe of Judah? Have you ever wondered that? Well, I'm going to tell you why.

In Genesis 49:8–12 we learn Judah was called the never-ending kingdom. Jacob blessed Judah and declared all would fall down and worship him. This is a prophecy of who Jesus would become. King David was also from Judah's bloodline. That is why the Scriptures tell us the throne of David shall be established before the Lord forever (1 Kings 2:45). *Judah* means "praise and thankfulness." So, Jesus is the Lion of the worshippers, and He expects to be worshipped.

Look at how John the Revelator describes Jesus in Revelation 5:4–5:

> I wept and wept and wept that no one was found able to open the scroll, able to read it. One of the Elders said, "Don't weep. Look—the Lion from Tribe Judah, the Root of David's Tree, has conquered. He can open the scroll, can rip through the seven seals."

The scroll is the title deed to earth, and God the Father was holding it. Who was worthy to open it? No one, so John wept! But in truth, the Lion of the tribe of Judah was able to open it because He had prevailed in His mission. He is the One worthy to receive our worship!

The Lion wept—will you?

I have always wanted to be one of God's lions in His kingdom. As a lion, I have found I am in a season of boldness and passion, but I have also learned these traits alone will not change the world. Boldness and passion are amazing, but I feel God increasingly calling me to brokenness and desperation. There is a call from heaven for the strong to be broken and the weak to shout.

Jesus represented brokenness on every level. He made up His mind that hurting humanity would know how He really felt. He didn't try to be manly or gruff. He allowed His feelings to show when He was broken and hurting. The shortest verse in the Bible, in fact, references Jesus's woundedness upon the death of His friend Lazarus. John 11:35 says, "Jesus wept" (NIV). The tears of Jesus prove His humanity to us. He is not a cold, lifeless Savior but One who is moved to tears.

Do you think Jesus didn't weep much? Really? Take a look at the following scripture:

> During the days of Jesus' life on earth, he offered up prayers and petitions with loud cries and tears to the one who could save him from death, and he was heard because of his reverent submission.
> —HEBREWS 5:7, NIV

Our Lion of the tribe of Judah was a weeping lion—so we must also be willing to weep.

We need to be broken.

Do you remember when King David had a very public moral failure? It ended up costing him everything. He was later restored, but in Psalm 51 he got very real when he said, "My sacrifice [the sacrifice acceptable] to God is a broken spirit; a broken and a contrite heart [broken down with sorrow for sin and humbly and thoroughly penitent], such, O God, You will not despise" (v. 17, AMP).

It was King David's brokenness that opened the door to his restoration. He was truly repentant, and he desired to be restored with God. The word *broken* used in Psalm 51:17

113

means "crushed, broken in pieces, torn, and brought to birth."
The word *contrite* means "collapsed physically or mentally."
These two words describe a soul in devastated brokenness.
John Piper describes the kind of brokenness we are meant
to have:

> A Christian is not a person who believes in his head
> the teachings of the Bible. Satan believes in his head
> the teachings of the Bible! A Christian is a person who
> has *died* with Christ, whose stiff neck has been broken,
> whose brazen forehead has been shattered, whose
> stony heart has been crushed, whose pride has been
> slain, and whose life is now mastered by Jesus Christ.[2]

Brokenness is a deep aching you feel when you are at the
end of yourself. Show me a person who is broken, and I will
show you someone God can use.

I have had occasions like this in my life. Many years ago I
battled deeply with insecurity on every level. I could preach
to thousands and still feel worthless. But the thing I have
learned about brokenness is that it usually leads to a type of
emotional breakdown—and this is a good thing.

That breakdown happened to me one night while I was in
a hotel room in Toronto, Canada. My son, Nate, had a terrible ear infection and begged for his daddy to come home.
The problem was that I was stuck in a snowstorm, and there
was no way to get home. The airport was shut down.

I felt like a failure as father, and those emotions got the best
of me. I found myself lying on a hotel room floor, weeping.
Little did I know this would be the night I would finally get
free and move forward. I remember weeping bitterly and
asking God to set me free. As I lay on the floor of the hotel
room, I cried out to God, saying, "Lord, I quit! I cannot continually travel the world preaching the gospel if You do not free
me." Suddenly I heard God say, "Pat, when will I be enough

for you? When will you allow Me to free you from your insecurity and fear?"

I said, "God, I want to be free. Please free me!" Then the Lord said, "You have to trust that I have your life and your family in My hands. Give Me your family! They are safer with Me than with you! Give Me your ministry. It is safer in My hands than in yours! Give Me your dreams! They are safer with Me than with you!" I said, "Lord, I give You everything!"

This was a supernatural breakthrough for me. I felt a resurrection spirit come over me. I suddenly stood to my feet and began to dance before the Lord in my hotel room. I had suffered for so long with that spirit of failure that I never realized what freedom felt like. Suddenly everything changed. It was as if I had put on a new pair of glasses. I could see clearly the hand of God in our life. My family noticed I was different. I was now secure in God. I wasn't ruled by my emotions. There would be many more times when I would have to remind myself that God was in charge, but this was a transformational moment. That night I learned the power of weeping.

You see, it wasn't until I was broken that God changed me. Sometimes the greatest thing that can happen to you is to get stuck by yourself—and if you don't believe that, just ask Jonah when you get to heaven!

The power of a lion's tears

I have come to believe it is impossible to have brokenness without also experiencing the power of our tears. That is why God said to me that we must become weeping lions. We all have to learn the power of weeping.

In the Bible we read that tears are the language of the soul. We read in 2 Kings 20:2–3, "Hezekiah turned his face to the wall and prayed to the LORD, 'Remember, O LORD, how I have walked before you faithfully and with wholehearted devotion and have done what is good in your eyes.' And Hezekiah wept bitterly" (NIV). Luke 7 records the account of Mary washing Jesus's feet with her tears.

God never ignores our tears. In fact, He even saves them in a bottle. That's right, your tears are in a bottle in heaven. Psalm 56:8 says, "You keep track of all my sorrows. You have collected all my tears in your bottle. You have recorded each one in your book" (NLT). Matthew Henry wrote of this verse, "God has a bottle and a book for his people's tears, both those for their sins and those for their afflictions....He observes them with compassion and tender concern; he is afflicted in their afflictions, and knows their souls in adversity."[3]

What makes you weep?

One spring afternoon, when my son was a junior in high school, I went to his football practice to watch from the sidelines. As I watched the practice, I could tell something wasn't right with Nate. He wasn't himself.

After practice was over, I told him I would see him when he got home. On my way home he called me from his cell phone. He was weeping uncontrollably. I told him to pull off the road and tell me what was going on. He had found out at school that two of his best friends had made some terrible choices while on spring break. They had given into temptation and even lost their virginity. They had both decided to no longer be Christians.

Nate was distraught. These were two friends who had stood with him as Christians. He said, "Dad, I feel like I have no one that will stand with me for Christ. I believed in these two friends so deeply."

After a while Nate was able to minister to one of those friends and lead him back to Christ. Weeks later that friend would show up at our house beaten and bruised by his mother's boyfriend, and Nate would help him stand tall again.

I believe there are times when God melts your heart. He takes you on a journey to brokenness. Many times those tears happen while you are in a valley. Psalm 84:5–7 says, "Blessed (happy, fortunate, to be envied) is the man whose strength is in

You, in whose heart are the highways to Zion. Passing through the Valley of Weeping (Baca), they make it a place of springs; the early rain also fills [the pools] with blessings. They go from strength to strength [increasing in victorious power]; each of them appears before God in Zion" (AMP). According to these verses, there is a valley of weeping. I think I have visited that valley on a few occasions, and what I have learned is that the valley of weeping always leads to streams of living water.

Repentance and brokenness come hand in hand. The Bible says, in 2 Corinthians 7:10, "Godly sorrow [tears] brings repentance that leads to salvation and leaves no regret, but worldly sorrow brings death" (NIV). It is when you become broken and allow God to fill the voids of your life that transformation takes place. It is in the broken and wounded places that God pours in His awesome healing.

Remember: "We have this treasure in jars of clay to show that this all-surpassing power is from God and not from us" (2 Cor. 4:7, NIV). I have found that when my jar of clay is cracked and broken, His glory can shine out of the cracks. Brokenness is a process of coming to a place of realizing that what we have considered a normal life of lost freedom is actually a life God didn't intend for us. Brokenness leads you to a new level of depth in the understanding of God's awesome character.

Be on guard in the jungle.

The world is spinning out of control and needs a church that will bring it back to repentance. A quote that has touched me deeply for years is from Leonard Ravenhill, who said, "Maybe, nay, surely we need ten days in an Upper Room or maybe more suitable for us a basement to mourn the departed glory, to apologize for our arrogance in preaching so long without a NATIONAL revival. The last revival mentioned in the Old Testament is found in the book of the prophet Joel. He proclaimed a solemn feast and said, 'Let the priests, the

ministers of the Lord, weep between the porch and the altar.'
Well, let's face it, who weeps anymore?"[4]

For years we have held church growth conferences and seminars that have helped grow local bodies of churches all across the world. Many times churches grow by swapping members, but only rarely do they grow by way of new conversions. I do believe, however, that we are in the season of mourning and weeping. As mentioned in an earlier chapter, Christians are being martyred every day for simply being followers of Christ. I believe that we are in what the Bible calls, in Matthew 24:8, "the beginning of sorrows" (NKJV).

If you do not have a strong foundation in Christ, you simply will not make it in this day. That means we need to have less success seminars and more times of getting back to the altar of repentance. If we are not careful, in our desire to see everyone blessed and prosperous, we will neglect the deepest characteristic of Christianity, and that is humility and brokenness. David Wilkerson once said, "The success philosophy preached today is a repackaged message from Norman Vincent Peale with few exceptions."[5]

The lion's den isn't safe.

So many times the church culture has operated as a place where the strong at heart blurt out their opinions while those tender of heart have sat on the sidelines, waiting in hope that someday they would get their turn. I believe there is a supernatural shift taking place in the church. That shift is for the quiet to rise up and speak and for the loud to weep. I believe God is awakening His leaders to our depravity, and that is why we must be remnant. We must become weeping lions who hear the cry of the roaring lambs.

Mass confusion has infiltrated the body. Many no longer fight for the unborn. We vote with our greed. We are careful to not call right from wrong so the wind of judgment doesn't shift in our direction. We rarely speak of Holy Spirit fire because we fear the masses won't like our vision of freedom.

We stand and declare who *we* are because we no longer have a revelation of who *He* is.

Please understand, I do believe that understanding and love for people are critical to touch lives. But in that we must be God's voice and not forgo biblical truth with conviction. We must not blur the lines between the world and those called to the cross of Jesus Christ. Enough is enough! The land is crying out for the wanderers on holy ground to arise with a holy passion and for the prowlers of Spirit to weep and wail.

I absolutely love passionate and alive services that are relevant, and I speak year-round at youth conferences that God is using to literally transform a generation. But I have often wondered if we are dangerously close to looking like a club. What do I mean? I mean that if we are simply producing services with no conviction—if we are churning out lots of cool atmosphere that does not lead people to transformation—would it not be better to just go to any downtown club in any major city? While I love to be in an atmosphere of excitement, lights, sound, and stage, that doesn't mean we ought to sacrifice truth for relevance. If we can combine a great atmosphere with a powerful encounter, then we will win. To sacrifice conviction for the thrill of an experience negates our purpose.

> The remnant has mastered the
> simple fact that true revival is
> not a gathering of the saved but
> a resurrection of the lost.

The remnant is called to be not only relevant but also revivalist. If we are not going to lead people to change, we may as well shut the doors. Malachi 1:10 reads, "'Oh, that one of you would shut the temple doors, so that you would not light useless fires on my altar! I am not pleased with you,' says the Lord Almighty, 'and I will accept no offering from your hands'" (NIV).

The safest place a person should be is in the house of God. That is why we call our places of worship "sanctuaries." We must allow the Holy Spirit to move freely and inhabit God's temples. You and I are the temple of the Holy Spirit (1 Cor. 6:19–20)! Our God inhabits our lives and makes them His home. God chooses to enter into us and thus produce a life of power, freedom, and authority. Without a Holy Spirit encounter, we will become dried-up religious institutions.

The invasion of the toothless lion

We will never change the world when do not allow God to first change our hearts. God never asked us to be like the world, but rather to invade the world with His light and truth. The problem is that just as the world no longer accepts truth, there is a faction of the church that has begun to only share partial truth. But half-truth is really no truth at all.

God has called us to declare a pure gospel. When we water down the gospel, we become the problem and not the answer. The apostle Paul spoke of standing firm in 2 Corinthians 2:16–17 when he said, "This is a terrific responsibility. Is anyone competent to take it on? No—but at least we don't take God's Word, water it down, and then take it to the streets to sell it cheap. We stand in Christ's presence when we speak; God looks us in the face. We get what we say straight from God and say it as honestly as we can."

There are leaders who have chosen to ignore that verse and water down the message. Maybe they have done this because they believe the Christian palate does not like it when the food is spicy. What do I mean? It is what the psalmist declared in Psalm 34:8: "Open your mouth and taste, open your eyes and see—how good God is. Blessed are you who run to him." People will lose their appetite if we change the taste of the gospel to a bland, watered-down version. God desires that we be hungry for more of Him! Jesus preached this in His powerful sermon on the Beatitudes: "You're blessed when you've worked up a good appetite for God. He's food and drink in the best meal you'll ever eat" (Matt. 5:6). The lions are starving for meat, but instead they are dining on milk.

The apostle Paul sent a warning to his protégé of the very things we are seeing today:

> In the presence of God and of Christ Jesus, who will judge the living and the dead, and in view of his appearing and his kingdom, I give you this charge: Preach the Word; be prepared in season and out of season; correct, rebuke and encourage—with great patience and careful instruction. For the time will come when men will not put up with sound doctrine. Instead, to suit their own desires, they will gather around them a great number of teachers to say what their itching ears want to hear. They will turn their ears away from the truth and turn aside to myths. But you, keep your head in all situations, endure hardship, do the work of an evangelist, discharge all the duties of your ministry.
> —2 Timothy 4:1–5, NIV

We must see the training ground of the called come alive again. The halls of many Christian universities are no longer filled with the sounds of deep spiritual intercourse of Scripture, nor are the chapels filled with a next generation longing to transform a world. Rather, we now hear the screaming sounds of compromise. Somewhere along the way we have bought into the idea that Scripture is no longer culturally relevant.

The remnant must make a stand. God's Word does not change with new seasons, new theories, or newly introduced agendas. In fact, God's Word has never bowed to kings, emperors, monarchies, or presidents of nations. God's Word will stand till the end as the ultimate source of truth and life.

When we lose our purpose as a church, we also begin to embrace passivity: "Does a lion roar in the forest if there's no carcass to devour? Does a young lion growl with pleasure if he hasn't caught his supper?" (Amos 3:4) The prophet Amos is asking why is it that we roar when we haven't really conquered anything. We have now seen the invasion of the "toothless lion." What is the toothless lion? It is very powerful presence with no bite.

We must get back to preaching the whole counsel of God. This is what the apostle Paul declared in Acts 20:27: "For I have not hesitated to proclaim to you the whole will of God" (NIV).

Grace anatomy

We are in a day when there are some kings of the jungles proclaiming a false grace message. Others are roaring like lions with a social gospel that has no accountability. Remember 2 Timothy 4:3–4: "For the time is coming when people will not endure sound teaching, but having itching ears they will accumulate for themselves teachers to suit their own passions, and will turn away from listening to the truth and wander off into myths" (ESV).

We now have a generation of leaders preaching that things such as consuming alcohol, cursing, and being a part of the world are fine as long as one practices moderation. I know some will say I am religious for taking a stand on social issues, but you see, I come from a family that was full of addicts and alcoholics. When my parents chose to follow Christ, He delivered them from all of the stuff that many are saying is now OK. I simply cannot go back to what destroyed my family for generations.

I am often asked whether I believe it is OK for people to consume alcohol. This question is often used as a litmus test to see whether I am "religious." It bothers me deeply when people make assumptions about me when they do not know why I take the stance I take. My family has been personally affected by alcoholism, and I refuse to give the enemy a door to entrap me or my children. Whenever I am asked about this, I always give the same unapologetic response. I begin by quoting the scripture "All things are lawful for me, but not all things are helpful; all things are lawful for me, but not all things edify" (1 Cor. 10:23, NKJV). Then I explain the reasons I do not consume alcohol:

1. My family history is marred by pain and addiction. I cannot open the door to something that nearly destroyed my family's lineage.

2. It is a proven fact that the next generation will always take freedoms to the next level. I have never wanted to give my children an excuse to consume alcohol in excess and end up getting killed in an accident or living a life of pain. I want to be the example to my children that removes all excuses.

3. I am not my own! First Corinthians 8:9 says, "Be careful, however, that the exercise of your freedom does not become a stumbling block to the weak" (NIV). Many people know me all over the world because of my travels preaching the gospel. I do not want to ruin the witness God has given me or be a stumbling block for anyone by consuming alcohol. Once while flying internationally the flight attendant poured me a glass of wine. The cabin of the plane was dark, so I did not notice she had poured this into my glass. Once I realized what happened, I asked her for something else to drink. When the plane landed and I gathered my belongings, a couple who had been on the plane came up to me and said, "We just saw you speak at a conference. We watched to see whether or not you were real. We want you to know we appreciate your witness for Christ." I said, "What do you mean?" They said, "We

watched you turn down alcohol on this flight.
That truly ministered to us, and we can't wait to
hear you this Sunday at our church." I thanked
them for their time and words, but most of all I
thanked Jesus that I had not hurt my witness.

God's Word demands separation. Jesus came with a sword
and not a feather. He even said He would divide the sheep
from the goats (Matt. 25:32). My heart's cry is that the remnant will realize we are the sheep. There must be a call to
either tell the truth or be quiet.

> O God, shatter their teeth in their mouth; break out
> the fangs of the young lions, O Lord.
>
> —Psalm 58:6, nas

The lion sleeps tonight.

Do you remember the song "The Lion Sleeps Tonight"? You
know, the song that talks about a mighty lion sleeping in the
jungle? I remember my family singing that song on car trips
when I was a kid. I never would have thought I'd someday
write about those lyrics in a book! Nevertheless, that song
describes what I believe has happened in Christianity.

Recently, while ministering in Singapore, I was asked the
same question by two key leaders within a twelve-hour span.
One of the leaders is known worldwide. Both said, "We are
very concerned about America and Australia." When I asked
them why, they both asked a question: "Who is preaching
truth in America?"

On both occasions I was too dumbfounded to respond. I
said I knew there were many preaching truth, but their voices
were not loud enough. Both leaders spoke of their concerns
about the doctrine of "hyper-grace" that is sweeping through
Singapore and into the western culture of the church.

In truth, this hyper-grace message has lulled many lions
in the church to sleep—while all lions need to learn to weep,

others need to first wake up. In this I am trying to say that very few voices speak up and stand tall for Jesus. My brothers and sisters, this should not be. We must be very careful that we are not embracing what I call "secular Christianity." Secular Christianity is an oxymoron. We act like the world in the name of Christ.

When we lose our desperation for more of Jesus, we lose our ability to distinguish what it means to have separation. We become complacent—and then we fall asleep. But Jesus didn't mince words. He said, "This is the verdict: Light has come into the world, but men loved darkness instead of light because their deeds were evil. Everyone who does evil hates the light, and will not come into the light for fear that his deeds will be exposed" (John 3:19–20, NIV). Jesus took it even further when He said, "And then many will be offended, will betray one another, and will hate one another. Then many false prophets will rise up and deceive many. And because lawlessness will abound, the love of many will grow cold" (Matt. 24:10–12, NKJV).

The remnant must be the opposite of lawlessness, as the spirit of the Antichrist is this lawlessness: "Don't let anyone deceive you in any way, for that day will not come until the rebellion occurs and the man of lawlessness is revealed, the man doomed to destruction. He will oppose and will exalt himself over everything that is called God or is worshiped, so that he sets himself up in God's temple, proclaiming himself to be God" (2 Thess. 2:3–4, NIV).

You may ask, "What is lawlessness?" The King James Bible uses the word *iniquity* in place of *lawlessness*. Both words simply mean "sin or rebellion against God." In 1 John 3:6 we see the same Greek the word again, but it is translated as *sinning*: "No one who lives in him keeps on sinning. No one who continues to sin has either seen him or known him" (NIV).

What happens when lawlessness invades the church? We succumb to the spirit of iniquity and begin to say compromise is OK. The hyper-grace movement is leading millions away from the cross into a dark land of such lawlessness. In this land compromise and complacency reign.

To be clear, I am not writing on this issue because I have embraced legalism over freedom. That couldn't be farther from the truth. I do not know where I would be without God's grace. I believe that with the message of the cross come unbelievable freedom and authority. One of my favorite verses is Romans 6:14: "For sin shall no longer be your master, because you are not under the law, but under grace" (NIV).

I do believe, however, that there is a need for balance when teaching on the subject of grace. Charles Spurgeon once said, "Discernment is not knowing the difference between right and wrong. It is knowing the difference between right and almost right."[6] Another way of saying it is what a dear pastor friend named Glenn Randall once said, "Compromised truths are lies distinguished as truth."

The message of grace without responsibility is running rampant in many circles today, and it has already lulled too many lions to sleep. Please understand, again, that I love and praise God for grace. The problem comes when we preach grace without repentance. That message will fill churches, but it will not fill heaven. Grace is the vehicle to freedom, but it does not give us a license to live like the world we are called to win. Titus 2:11–14 (NIV) lays it out pretty clearly:

> For the grace of God that brings salvation has appeared to all men. It teaches us to say "No" to ungodliness and worldly passions, and to live self-controlled, upright and godly lives in this present age, while we wait for the blessed hope—the glorious appearing of our great God and Savior, Jesus Christ, who gave himself for us to redeem us from all wickedness and to purify for himself a people that are his very own, eager to do what is good.

The Bible declares that grace was extended to pull us out of sin, not to allow us to continue to wallow in it. Does that mean we are supposed to be perfect? No. God doesn't expect us to be perfect, but He does expect us to stay in pursuit of Him. This means we must be awake and on guard.

The grace message that permeates churches today is almost right. Yes, grace does pardon and set us free—but we must continue to walk out that freedom through our relationship with Christ. Why? Because the freedom Christ brings keeps us from a life of sin. The church is not a social club gathering of those who have learned to avoid the law for their own gain. It is not a place to relax and lose focus. Rather, the Bible speaks clearly about our need to grow up in Christ:

> No prolonged infancies among us, please. We'll not tolerate babes in the woods, small children who are an easy mark for impostors. God wants us to grow up, to know the whole truth and tell it in love—like Christ in everything. We take our lead from Christ, who is the source of everything we do. He keeps us in step with each other. His very breath and blood flow through us, nourishing us so that we will grow up healthy in God, robust in love.
>
> —EPHESIANS 4:14–16

I am reminded of what the great preacher Dietrich Bonhoeffer wrote about grace in his classic book *The Cost of Discipleship,* which was published in 1937 during the height of Hitler's Nazi Germany: "Cheap grace is the preaching of forgiveness without requiring repentance, baptism without church discipline, Communion without confession....Cheap grace is grace without discipleship, grace without the cross, grace without Jesus Christ."[7] The apostle Bill Johnson, from Bethel Church in Redding, California, speaks of grace in a profound way. He says, "Grace doesn't excuse sin; it empowers righteousness. Grace doesn't overlook sin; it empowers obedience."[8] The apostle Paul wrote of "the true grace of God" in 1 Peter 5:12 (NIV). He said we must not receive that grace in vain (2 Cor. 6:1).

We must preach grace as God's arm extended toward freedom and not God's eyes shutting as we continue in sin. True freedom comes when we walk out repentance and don't treat grace as a license to keep on sinning. Christ's cross was enough to satisfy your heart and keep you. That doesn't mean we abuse the grace afforded to us.

We must be careful about listening to the wrong voices about grace, just as Jude warned long ago: "For certain men whose condemnation was written about long ago have secretly slipped in among you. They are godless men, who pervert the grace of our God into a license for immorality and deny Jesus Christ our only Sovereign and Lord" (Jude 4, NIV).

This message is not easy to share, but I love this generation enough to share the truth. God's grace was given to us to empower us to become a new creation. That is why we are called to not conform to this world but to renew our minds every day (Rom. 12:2). The hyper-grace message allows the old man to coexist with the new man. I know we all battle with our sin nature, but we as Christians are called to be continually transformed by God's power.

The hyper-grace teaching comes extremely close to the false teaching of universalism, which says Christ paid the price on the cross, making us free to do what we want. Here is another definition: "In Christianity, universal reconciliation is the doctrine that all sinful and alienated human souls—because of divine love and mercy—will ultimately be reconciled to God."9

Romans 10:9 tells us, however, that in order to be saved you must "confess with your mouth, 'Jesus is Lord,' and believe in your heart that God raised him from the dead, you will be saved." Yes, Christ paid for our sins at the cross, but we must accept Him as Lord to be saved.

There are even some Christian leaders today who teach there is no need for conviction. Why, then, did Jesus say to the churches of Revelation that they must repent? Revelation 2:4–5 says, "But you walked away from your first love—why? What's going on with you, anyway? Do you have any idea how far you've fallen? A Lucifer fall! Turn back! Recover your dear early love. No time to waste, for I'm well on my way to removing your light from the golden circle." God offers us His grace to make us better, not to make us like Satan. We must redig the ancient wells of truth. When men have stumbled in the dark in previous eras, they needed to go back to the early precepts. God's Word is our precept.

This is why the lions must wake and weep again. I believe God will use the remnant to awaken our nation from its slumber. We must be willing to declare what Leonard Ravenhill said: "America needs a Joan of Arc. The British need another Boadicea to wage war on her immorality. Both nations need another Jeremiah to weep over their sins, another John the Baptist to call them to repentance, and another Elijah to bring fire down from heaven that the multitude may cry again, 'The LORD, He is God! The LORD, HE is God!'"[10]

We are living in a time when the remnant must rise. We have been quiet too long. We must see the lions gain their strength through God again. God is ready to refresh the lions—and the greatest way to refresh the lions is for them to hear the roaring of the lambs!

ROARING LAMBS

I once heard an awesome line in the movie *Robin Hood* that starred Russell Crowe: "Rise and rise again until lambs become lions."[11] It means never give up for the cause of liberty—never, ever give up. Rise and rise again, until the docile lambs become conquering lions. That is what we must do.

No matter how many times we fall down, we must be like Jesus and get back up. Jesus died as a lamb but rose as a lion!

And He died as our Lamb, in fact, so we could roar like lions too. We've just learned Jesus is the Lion of the tribe of Judah, yes. But He is also the Lamb of God—and we must hear the roaring of that Lamb!

Let's explore that Lamb's roar so we can learn to be the roaring remnant that's sorely needed now.

Shepherds seek the Lamb.

It is the job of shepherds to search out lambs that are lost or have wandered off. God always uses shepherds. Look at Moses and David in the Bible; they were both shepherds when they received their marching orders. The same thing happened the night Jesus was born—it was the shepherds who found Jesus. In essence, they were searching not for a lost lamb, but rather a lamb that would save them.

The shepherds were probably running and weeping at one and the same time because we needed a lamb to rescue the world. Can you imagine the scene as they arrived at the stable? They could hear the animals. They could feel the excitement in the atmosphere. And as they looked closer, there lay a King. A lamb and lion at one and the same time! I imagine when baby Jesus let out a cry, it shook the heavenlies and put hell on alert!

Disciples declare the Lamb.

John the Baptist represents the remnant. He was sent to prepare the way for Jesus. One day he was standing in the Jordan River baptizing people when he saw Jesus approach. "Look, the Lamb of God, who takes away the sin of the world," he cried (John 1:29, NIV). Then the next day he declared it again: "The next day John was there again with two of his disciples. When he saw Jesus passing by, he said, 'Look, the Lamb of God!' When the two disciples heard him say this, they followed Jesus" (vv. 35–37, NIV).

John understood that his sole purpose in life was to be a PR person for Jesus. He was sent to prepare the way for the

Lamb of God. John understood that he had to decrease so that Christ must increase. He even allowed his disciples to leave him and follow Jesus. The role of a disciple is to always point people back to the cross. If we keep this mind-set at all times, then we will never make ministry about ourselves. Everywhere we go we must point people to Jesus. He is the only one who can set people free.

Jesus is our power source and our message. When we pray for people, we must realize that we are a conduit of His power. In other words, we are the go-between. For years I thought that I was a part of making the miracle happen. I thought I needed to be super-spiritual in order for God to use me to see people saved, healed, or delivered. Then I realized that if I would just get out of the way, God could use me. When we minister, we are simply the hands of God extended. Our hands must always point to Jesus and away from our personalities, positions, and platform. When I finally realized it wasn't about me, I began to see miracles. We touch people's lives when we first touch the Savior's heart. We are the modern-day town criers! If we simply declare that Jesus's presence is here, He will do the rest!

Slaughter of the Lamb

When the time came for His crucifixion, the Lamb was naked, ridiculed, beaten, tortured, and led away for us. Isaiah 53:7 says, "He was oppressed and afflicted, yet he did not open his mouth; he was led like a lamb to the slaughter, and as a sheep before her shearers is silent, so he did not open his mouth" (NIV). Matthew 27:31 says, "After they had mocked him, they took off the robe and put his own clothes on him. Then they led him away to crucify him" (NIV).

As Jesus hung on the cross for our sins, He became the ultimate sacrifice. Matthew 27:45–46 says, "From the sixth hour until the ninth hour darkness came over all the land. About the ninth hour Jesus cried out in a loud voice, *"Eloi, Eloi, lama sabachthani?"*—which means "My God, my God, why have you forsaken me?" (NIV).

The Lamb was in such agonizing pain! His Father turned His back on Him because He couldn't bear to see His Son in such agony, nor could He look upon our sin that was now upon His Son.

But the Lamb was not finished. The Lamb roared for you and me! Matthew 27:50 says, "And when Jesus had cried out again in a loud voice, he gave up his spirit" (NIV).

Feed the lambs

The disciples scattered when Jesus died. Simon Peter, whose name means "rock," even betrayed Jesus as He stood trial before the Sanhedrin. That great future lion of the New Testament church was broken for his failure to be loyal to Jesus.

We know Jesus resurrected on the third day. Then He went and found the disciples fishing. He stood on the banks of the river and called out to them. The disciple John realized it was Jesus first, but Peter is the one who dove out of his boat and swam to the shore. When he arrived, Jesus had already cooked him breakfast, and they began to have one of the greatest talks in history. John 21:15–16 gives us the account:

> After breakfast, Jesus said to Simon Peter, "Simon, son of John, do you love me more than these?" "Yes, Master, you know I love you." Jesus said, "Feed my lambs." He then asked a second time, "Simon, son of John, do you love me?" "Yes, Master, you know I love you." Jesus said, "Shepherd my sheep."

This is the moment Peter received his commission to rise above his past failures and lead like a lion. To do so, he must feed the lambs. Why? Because the lamb bleats the loudest when it is hungry. Jesus was saying, "You were a weeping lion, but now feed the roaring lambs."

We too must get back to weeping, for the lambs are roaring. They are hungry! Remnant, we must weep and then rise as lions!

Chapter 9

ARE YOU LIKE HIM?

Hate evil and love good, then work it out in the
public square. Maybe GOD, the God-of-the-Angel-
Armies, will notice your remnant and be gracious.

—AMOS 5:15

Dear Remnant,
Do you look like Jesus? It's time to be
His image to a world looking for a Savior.
We are called to be the representative of
Him.

I WANT TO SHARE with you a story of something that took place a couple of years ago. I was sitting on a long flight, and it had been a very long and trying day. I think everything that could go wrong had gone wrong, from flight delays to encountering rude people and so on. I had not been so nice to the people I had encountered.

While sitting on a flight that afternoon, I tried having a time of prayer. I knew when I got off of the flight, I would have to go speak at a youth conference. I did not feel very prepared.

My prayer time was really just a time spent whining. And then I heard the Lord speak to me.

"Pat, do you look like Me?" he asked.

"What do You mean?" I responded.

"Do you look like Me? Are you a good representative of Me?"

As I heard those words, I began to weep. Eventually I choked out, "No, Lord, I don't think I do."

He then spoke to me these words: "I need you to look like Me if you are going to be My representative."

Do You Look Like Him?

I don't always look like Jesus. But the Bible tells us we're supposed to be just like Him. Romans 8:29 says, "For those God foreknew he also predestined to be conformed to the likeness of his Son, that he might be the firstborn among many brothers" (NIV). That word *likeness* in the Greek is *eikone*. It is where we get the word *icon*. The word *icon* means "image, resemblance, profile, or representative."

> The remnant has chosen to be the
> least of these to the greatest of them.

I can't help but think of the many times I have been a terrible example of the icon or image of Jesus. I call it "losing your witness" as a representative of Christ. Nearly every time I have lost my witness, it was during a season of weariness or offense.

I am reminded of the time I confronted a man at a hotel desk in Alaska for parking in the doorway. There was ice on the ground, and my family had to slip and slide through the parking lot because the man behind the desk had blocked the entrance. By the time I got to the counter, I was irate. After finding out it was actually the desk clerk's car, I began to berate him. I heard Karen say, in the midst of my rant, "Come on, Nate. Let's go to the room." My son, Nate, then said, "Hold on, Mom. I want to see Dad give it to him."

I froze in my tracks. I realized in that moment that I had been a complete jerk. I apologized profusely to the man and went up to the room with my family. Once in the room, I washed my family's feet. Then I went back down to the lobby and apologized again to the guy behind the counter.

I have made many mistakes like this. I have ruined my witness more than a few times. But Jesus never ruined His witness. Sure, He got angry and frustrated, but He always remained true to the calling of a servant.

That day, sitting on the flight and hearing God say to me, "Pat, do you look like Me?"—well, it impacted me in a profound way. I decided to do a study on the character of Jesus in order to know what it means to look like Him. This became a place of awakening for me, for it taught me that God has created me to represent His Son.

GETTING TO KNOW JESUS

I never knew Jesus as a friend growing up. To me, Jesus was simply too majestic and impersonal for me to really know Him. Most of the time I saw Him as either a baby in a manger or an angry king on a horse. I heard rules growing up—do this and don't do that! I knew my parents knew Jesus, but I never really thought of Him as more than a mandate in our house.

But I wanted to know Him so bad. Even as a young boy I begged to see Him during dark nights and long altar call experiences. Then one day I had an encounter. My dad pastored a little church in Alabama, and every year we would go to an Assemblies of God youth camp in Clanton, Alabama. This was always a highlight of our year because my dad would spend the whole week with my brother, sister, and me. This particular year, when the evangelist gave an altar call I went forward. All I remember is crying all the way to the altar. I didn't know why, but all I could do was cry. My dad came and sat beside me at the altar, and I laid my head in his lap. For several hours I cried and wept as the presence of God swept over me. This is the night I was saved and filled with the Spirit.

I have had many encounters since then, but becoming like Jesus is a continual journey. The closer we grow to Him, the more we reflect Him. The Apostle Paul addressed this when talking to the church at Corinth:

> Whenever, though, they turn to face God as Moses did, God removes the veil and there they are—face-to-face! They suddenly recognize that God is a living, personal presence, not a piece of chiseled stone. And when God is personally present, a living Spirit, that old, constricting legislation is recognized as obsolete. We're free of it! All of us! Nothing between us and God, our faces shining with the brightness of his face. And so we are transfigured much like the Messiah, our lives gradually becoming brighter and more beautiful as God enters our lives and we become like him.
>
> —2 CORINTHIANS 3:18–20

Beholding Jesus changes us. What does that mean? It means the more time you spend with Him, the more you will take on His attributes. The more God gets in you, the more transformed you become. You literally begin to be the embodiment of Jesus to the world.

CALLED TO BE HIS EXAMPLE

It's good to know that the more we know Jesus, the more we become like Him—because, after all, God has called us to be His representative. Paul wrote about this in 2 Corinthians 5:20: "So we are Christ's ambassadors, God making His appeal as it were through us. We [as Christ's personal representatives] beg you for His sake to lay hold of the divine favor [now offered you] and be reconciled to God" (AMP).

> The remnant understands the fruit of the Spirit is not a salad for a church potluck but rather the diet of a lifetime.

That means we are meant to be Christ's example to the world. This may be difficult to understand, but here's the truth of it: we are asked to emulate a King who chose to be a pauper. The confining of a Prince in the body of a pauper allowed my King to be in touch with every pain and hurt we face. Here is proof: "For you know the grace of our Lord Jesus Christ, that though he was rich, yet for your sake he became poor, so that you through his poverty might become rich" (2 Cor. 8:9, NIV).

Jesus came wrapped in the humanity of flesh and pain yet retained His divinity in order to be the spotless sacrifice. He did this to prove that we could know the power of being remnant. God has called us to look like His Son, and Jesus was the personification of what it means to be remnant. He was every definition of remnant you can imagine.

SEEING JESUS

I've always been perplexed by what the Bible says about our being made in the image of God (Gen. 1:27). I know God put me together, but how do I actually look like Him—bear His image?

And yet, considering my track record, I think the greater question probably is: How could *I* be chosen to be an ambassador of Christ? I mean, *me*—really? Why would God choose me to represent the King of all creation? Jesus is our consolation. He is our answer. How in the world can I be like that?

Again we come back to this truth: if we are to look and be like Jesus, we must know Him. So the first revelation we, the remnant, must understand is *who Jesus is*. You have to understand who Jesus was as a person in order to look like Him.

And believe it or not, Jesus is not just found in the New Testament. That's right; He can be seen all through the Old Testament. There are times where He is present directly in Scripture, and other times He is represented by a shadow and type. He is holding a sword at the entrance of a garden.

He is represented by a boy on a mountain about to be sacrificed. He is the fourth man in a fire. Sometimes He is the pillow for a prophet. Other times He is a brook that dries up after three years. Sometimes He is a stone in a sling; other times He is a prophet whose wife is a harlot. He has always been in the picture; we just don't always see Him.

It is hard to see Jesus in our daily walk sometimes, even though we can see Him clearly in Scripture. And so one of the questions I ask myself all the time is: Can I see God at work in my life? This is critical because if you can't see Jesus at work in your life, you will reduce Him to a symbol. Sometimes our issues are so big that we can't see Him in the midst of our "now."

ENCOUNTERING JESUS

Speaking of seeing Jesus in the midst of our "now," let me tell you a story of one way that happened to me. Early one morning I sat in our den doing my devotions. I had flown in late the night before and was very tired. God had poured out His Spirit in the services where I'd ministered, but it had felt like more of a spiritual war than normal. So this was one of those mornings where I really needed an encounter with Jesus.

Karen was leaving to take Abby to school and reminded me that when she got home, we were going to work out together. We had been doing a workout program called Insanity. Trust me, it is insane. She told me she had put a protein and fruit shake in the refrigerator for me, and I grudgingly told her I would be ready.

As I sat in my chair praying, I said, "Lord, I really need a personal encounter today." I finished my morning devotions and turned on the morning news for a few moments. A few minutes later I made my way to the kitchen to get my protein drink, and as I reached for the refrigerator door, I had a very powerful encounter with Jesus. I was suddenly overwhelmed with His love. It was as if He had invaded our kitchen. It really is hard to describe. In my weariness He overwhelmed me. I found myself sitting in the floor weeping! The presence of God overtook me for what seemed like an hour, but it was really only a few minutes. It was as if all Jesus was waiting for me to do was simply ask Him for an encounter. When Karen came in from taking Abby to school, she could feel the presence of God in our kitchen. I told her, "God just met with me!" And we both immediately went to prayer.

I honestly believe every need you and I have can be met with these simple Jesus encounters.

THEY WANT TO SEE JESUS

The world is looking for a Savior. Why do you think the top movies at the box office are about superheroes? It is because of man's deep cry to be rescued. The problem is that we live in a day where the person of Jesus is reduced to man's concepts and reasoning. The world wants to see Jesus—they just don't know they want to.

As I have traveled the world, I have made note of what people, cities, regions, and cultures think of God. Below is a list of what I believe Jesus is to so many (but please don't let the list below offend you; I realize there are many exceptions to the rule):

- In the southern United States He is reduced to a symbol of culture.

- In the northern United States He is an icon on holidays.

- In the midwestern United States He is an interruption to daily routine.

- In the western United States He is a mystical figure.

- In Salt Lake City He is older brother, just a notch higher than Joseph Smith.

- In Miami He is a mixture of Catholicism and voodoo, a gold statue encased in glass in the front yard of someone's home.
- In Montreal He is a symbol of religion and a concrete moneybox in a cathedral.
- On the west and east coasts of the United States He is a symbol of oppression to self-expression.
- In Hollywood He is an idiot, a curse word, a wimp, and a racist.
- In Washington DC He is an ideologue, a red neck, and a lobbyist.
- In Saudi Arabia He is just another prophet.
- In Europe He is just another way to heaven.
- In New York He is a curse word.
- In China He is forbidden.
- In Russia He is a hidden statue in a cold, isolated land.
- In Burma He is unknown.
- In India He is one of many gods.
- In schools He is the minimized icon you can get sued or expelled over.
- On Wall Street He is an off-shore account.
- In some churches He used to move mightily.
- In some youth ministries He is a fifteen-minute talk so we can get to the games.
- In the backseats of cars He is ignored.
- At the movies He gets on our nerves because conviction requires action.
- In politics He is a voting bloc.

We must realize Jesus is more than just an ideology. To me He is Savior and redeemer, rescuer and peace. In our darkness

He is the one who hears and receives our weeping. In our tiredness He is our strength. In our despair He is our comforter.

WHAT JESUS LOOKS LIKE

So, let's talk about what Jesus looks like. For starters, He looks like a lamb. He is the Lamb of God—a lamb who was seen first in Genesis covering the nakedness of man. As the Lamb grew, He became a male child—the blood of the lamb on a doorpost to rescue Israel from bondage. Later He was the spotless lamb (1 Pet. 1:19)—the perfect Lamb whose blood would not only cover us but also become personal by cleansing us.

The prophet Isaiah declared that the Lamb is not really a lamb but a man: "He was oppressed and afflicted, yet he did not open his mouth; he was led like a lamb to the slaughter, and as a sheep before her shearers is silent, so he did not open his mouth" (Isa. 53:7, NIV). Then, all of a sudden, a crazy preacher by the name of John the Baptist who was standing in a muddy river declared Him to be the "Lamb of God, who takes away the sin of the world" (John 1:29, NIV).

After John's declaration, the Lamb of God took center stage. The entire Old Testament planned it out, and the New Testament brought it together in a dramatic tone. Jesus couldn't come as God, for that would have blown us away. His heavenly glory would have blinded us and forced a response. Instead, He wanted us to have free will to accept our Savior or not.

And so He reduced to a seed and grew as a baby in a womb. God was in a womb! Can you believe it? Because of that, Jesus knows what it is like to grow while hiding in order to become something great. He gave up the heavenlies to become our Savior. He gave up the ability to travel through time and thought. He gave up the greatest worship ever—that of the angels. He gave up glory to become nothing. And He faced discouragement, pain, suffering, humiliation, weariness, fear, and loneliness—all this for you and me. He humbled Himself so He could be touched by the feelings of our infirmities (Heb. 4:15).

Jesus began His ministry by turning water to wine. He would then heal leprosy, raise a dead girl, create a meal with two fish and five loaves for thousands, spit in the eyes of a blind man, drive out demons and make demons bow, rescue an adulterous woman from the religious, encounter a woman in need at a well, preach in the synagogue, overturn the tables, curse a tree with no fruit, and do many more miracles. Yet all of that was part of a process—a process that would lead Him to the cross for you and me.

When He began readying Himself to go to the cross, He rebuked everyone who tried to stop Him. Jesus said, "I have to do this. I must fulfill what I was sent to do!" (See Matthew 16:23.) Then He was led away to die.

Jesus became human so He could accomplish the impossible feat of stepping out of glory into a harsh and dying world. Philippians 2:8 says, "And being found in appearance as a man, he humbled himself and became obedient to death—even death on a cross!" (NIV). He became our mediator (1 Tim. 2:5–6). That means He became the middleman. He became the lowest of the low for us (2 Cor. 8:8–9).

All these things should absolutely stir you up. You were so important that Jesus did all of this for you!

But do you look like Him?

I ask you this because if you are truly going to be remnant, you must look like Jesus. Remember that one definition of *remnant* is "a small piece of cloth left on the bolt after the rest is gone." Jesus has returned to His Father, physically gone from the earth, but the remnant looks like what—or who, in this case—is gone. You must look like the original to be a remnant. And Jesus was the true representative of remnant. Do you look like Him?

IT'S GOING TO COST SOMETHING

I must warn you that once you begin to look like Jesus, things may get very tough. The more you look like Him, the more persecution you will receive:

> If you're abused because of Christ, count yourself fortunate. It's the Spirit of God and his glory in you that brought you to the notice of others. If they're on you because you broke the law or disturbed the peace, that's a different matter. But if it's because you're a Christian, don't give it a second thought. Be proud of the distinguished status reflected in that name!
>
> —1 PETER 4:14–16

A dear friend who pastors a church in New Mexico sent me a text to ask me to pray for his two sons. Both of his sons were under great persecution for making a stand as Christians on their campuses. I began to pray for each of them. A couple days later God told me to get their phone numbers and text them. I wrote them both a simple text: "I am so proud of you. God has chosen you to be His voice to a hurting world. Stand strong and don't bow to culture. God is raising you up as a remnant." A couple weeks later one of the young men wrote me a long text. In his text he explained how God was now using him on his football team to lead halftime prayer. This young man is a great athlete. He shared that his team now looked to him as a leader. He even used the story of David and Goliath to motivate his team. His team then defeated one of the best teams in a region! The whole team kept declaring during the game, "We are Davids!"

My goal was to push them forward.

There is such a battle to make each of us come into alignment with the world. But we must stand firm even when persecution comes. Someone once said, "If you don't stand for something, you will fall for anything." You were not put here to appease the world or belong to its mind-set. You were created for one thing, and that is to bring praise to God.

143

Four Ways to Embody Jesus

As the remnant, we must possess four distinct characteristics of Christ to be relevant to a dying world. If you are going to be the voice of Jesus and His representative in this generation, you must possess these attitudes—purity, compassion, a servant's heart, and authority.

1. Purity—it allows you to see God

There is an onslaught from the enemy to keep a generation bound to lust and perversion. We live in a time where you can access porn on your phone and see it on billboards. But this kind of onslaught isn't new! Our enemy approached Adam and Eve, and he holds the apple out to you too. You have to decide what kind of life you want to live—an imaginary one, or a life of purpose.

Jesus was the purest man to ever live. He showed us you can be in this world but not of it. Jesus desires for you and me to also live that type of life. The remnant are those who say no to the world and yes to the cross.

Purity is not only relevant to your convictions; one person's ideas of purity may be very different from another's. That is why God gave us His Word as a guideline. What I call pure you may call legalism, but the truth is not negotiable. You don't decide what is pure—God does!

I have spoken to hundreds of thousands of young people across the world, and I have found the most difficult battle facing this generation is that of staying pure. They must get God's road map and use it. His road map is the Bible. The Bible brings maturity in every area.

Jesus gave us a powerful command in Matthew 5:8, "Blessed are the pure in heart for they will see God" (NIV). The Greek word for "pure" is *katharos*. It means "to be free from corrupt desire. To be free from sin and guilt and free from every admixture of what is false. To be blameless, innocent." Another definition even means "to be purified by fire." If you have faced some fire lately, that just means you're getting purified.

God says if you want to see Him, you must get clean and restored. Here is Matthew 5:8 in *The Message* Bible: "You're blessed when you get your inside world—your mind and heart—put right. Then you can see God in the outside world." You will never see the world through God's glasses without cleaning up your life. Then you will have a whole new vision. You will suddenly see someone from the opposite sex not as someone to be desired but rather as someone to whom you can minister.

God can so transform your thinking that the thought of perversion makes you sick. The psalmist declared in Psalm 101:3, "I will set before my eyes no vile thing. The deeds of faithless men I hate; they will not cling to me" (NIV).

In the oldest book of the Bible Job says, "I made a solemn pact with myself never to undress a girl with my eyes. So what can I expect from God? What do I deserve from God Almighty above? Isn't calamity reserved for the wicked? Isn't disaster supposed to strike those who do wrong? Isn't God looking, observing how I live? Doesn't he mark every step I take?" (Job 31:1–4). There is more truth in this one small passage than most can handle. Some versions say Job made a covenant with his eyes. That is so powerful! He made a pact with his very eyes that he would be careful where he looked and what he looked at. Job had every reason to try and fulfill his flesh. He was lonely, weary, and heartsick, yet he stood tall.

In an even greater way Jesus represented purity at every level. He never allowed Himself to be taken in by the enemy—and boy, the enemy sure tried! It is recorded in Matthew 4 that Jesus fought every temptation for you. All three temptations He faced represent every sin we could possibly fall into. We even have a promise that He will always provide an exit door when we seem backed into a corner of sin: "No test or temptation that comes your way is beyond the course of what others have had to face. All you need to remember is that God will never let you down; he'll never let you be pushed past your limit; he'll always be there to help you come through it" (1 Cor. 10:13).

Your body belongs to God before it belongs to anyone else. Your purity has value! More than that, you have to realize you are a temple and not a shack. You are not for sale. Jesus already bought you with a price, so we have to honor God with our bodies (1 Cor. 6:20).

We are remnant, and being the remnant of God means choosing a life separate from what the world considers normal. He loves you too much to let you be used by the world. Jesus understood purity, and He will marry a bride someday—you and me, His church. He deserves a bride who saved herself for her wedding day. Does that mean we are perfect? No. Remember, He doesn't demand perfection but pursuit. That is what matters most—that you would seek to be like Jesus in all purity.

2. Compassion—be passionate about it

Compassion is a characteristic the world has not experienced very often from the church. This is a tough one, because most of us have had compassion and it resulted in disappointment. So many times we offer help only to find out we have been duped or someone's motives were wrong. Yet we must never stop bringing hope even if it means getting hurt in the process.

We must keep our hearts open to the hurting. Compassion is the yearning to help those in need. It is the compelling sense that you want to fix the things that hurt your heart. It is the nagging feeling of "I must do more" or "I could have done more."

It is what separates you from the way most of the world thinks. The word *compassion* means "a feeling of deep sympathy and sorrow for another who is stricken by misfortune, accompanied by a strong desire to alleviate the suffering." It is a deep pulling from within to step up and fix things.

The Greek word for "compassion" is *splagchnizomai*. That

sounds like a crazy word—try saying it five times fast! But its meaning is so powerful. It means "to have the bowels yearn, or an inward deep affliction." In other words, you feel something so deeply that you ache.

Karen, Nate, and I felt this way as we drove the streets of Beijing to get our daughter. We looked out the windows of a bus and at times could not even speak as we saw the hurting and poor on the streets. I have also felt this deep inner pain when a student or adult tells me his or her history. There have been times where students have walked up to me and said, "I wish you were my dad." They would then share they either had no relationship with their father or that their father was abusive.

I do not believe that you can truly be called to lost humanity without a deep compassion for the hurting. Compassion gives you a desire to help instead of judge. It also causes you not to think more highly of yourself than you should. When you place others first, you create an atmosphere for healing.

The practice of compassion increases our capacity to care. It reinforces charity, empathy, and sympathy. It is a very good exercise for your heart muscle. Paul mentions compassion when speaking to the Philippian church in Philippians 2:1–2: "If you have any encouragement from being united with Christ, if any comfort from his love, if any fellowship with the Spirit, if any tenderness and compassion, then make my joy complete by being like-minded, having the same love, being one in spirit and purpose" (NIV). Paul is saying that when you align yourself with God's Spirit, then compassion will flow forth with much joy.

One of my favorite quotes is attributed to St. Augustine: "Hope has two beautiful daughters; their names are Anger and Courage. Anger at the way things are, and Courage to see that they do not remain the way they are."[1] This quote inspires me to get up and do something for others.

The world is hurting, and we are called to carry life and light to this world. The best way to invade darkness is with a candle of hope and the bread of life. James teaches us what this looks like:

> Anyone who sets himself up as "religious" by talking a good game is self-deceived. This kind of religion is hot air and only hot air. Real religion, the kind that passes muster before God the Father, is this: Reach out to the homeless and loveless in their plight, and guard against corruption from the godless world.
>
> —James 1:26–27

Jesus went out of His way to go to the hurting. He actually avoided the religious. He went where He could be of service. In the ministry of Jesus we learn, "Jesus went through all the towns and villages, teaching in their synagogues, preaching the good news of the kingdom and healing every disease and sickness. When he saw the crowds, he had compassion on them, because they were harassed and helpless, like sheep without a shepherd" (Matt. 9:35–36, NIV). Matthew 14:14 also mentions His compassion: "When Jesus landed and saw a large crowd, he had compassion on them and healed their sick" (NIV).

My life was radically changed on October 27, 2013. I was ministering at a powerful church in Roanoke, Virginia. That night I shared my message "Why Is God So Mad at Me?" The altars were filled with hungry people who found healing in the arms of a loving Savior. After the service I stood in the foyer of the church at our ministry table. The pastor's wife brought a couple and their teenage daughter to meet me. She explained that the parents had been through a very dark season because their nineteen-year-old son had been killed in an accident several weeks earlier.

I turned to the couple and took the mother by the hands. I said, "I cannot imagine your pain." Instantly I had a vision. I found myself standing in the throne room of heaven. I could see a very tall, lanky young man worshipping God with his arms stretched out in praise. I also saw that the young man was wearing a plaid shirt. Immediately I came back and found myself looking into the eyes of the parents. I said, "Can I tell you something that just happened?" They said, "Sure." I asked them, "Is your son tall and skinny?" They said, "Oh, yes, he is very tall and skinny." I then said, "I know this is weird, but did your son wear a plaid shirt?"

The mother stepped back and almost fell over. Their daughter suddenly said, "Yes! A red one! He loved that shirt! I go in his room and smell it all the time!" I then said, "I just saw him worshipping in heaven!" The family began to weep. The mother fell to the ground and began to worship the Lord. This moment of compassion opened the door to an amazing moment. God is looking for people who will walk in compassion. If we will walk in compassion, it will remove our desire to be seen, and Jesus will be revealed.

What really inspires me concerning our Lord is that He didn't hide His emotions. He proved to us a man could have a soft heart and a pure mind. Jesus was all about ministering to and loving those in need. Are you like Him?

3. Service—make it your style

What truly separates Jesus from every other king is not only His divinity but also His servant posture. When kings rode white stallions, He rode a donkey. When kings slept in the palace, He slept on a hillside or in a boat. He confounded everyone because He refused to be what everyone expected. Here it is in black and white—Jesus came to serve:

> Your attitude should be the same as that of Christ Jesus: Who, being in very nature God, did not consider equality with God something to be grasped, but made himself nothing, taking the very nature of a servant, being made in human likeness. And being found in appearance as a man, he humbled himself and became obedient to death—even death on a cross!
>
> —PHILIPPIANS 2:5–8, NIV

Jesus gave away everything He had. He presented to the world a Savior who had only one desire, and that was to see mankind set free. He spent His days hanging out with sinners and the hurting. He continually challenged the political system because they couldn't get a handle on Him. They thought to themselves, "What makes this guy tick?" He couldn't be bought or bribed. Even His own disciples thought He was supposed to tear up the Roman Empire!

Then, as His exit from the earth was nearing, He did the unthinkable. He wrapped a towel around His waist and started washing the disciples' feet:

> Jesus knew that the Father had put all things under his power, and that he had come from God and was returning to God; so he got up from the meal, took off his outer clothing, and wrapped a towel around his waist. After that, he poured water into a basin and began to wash his disciples' feet, drying them with the towel that was wrapped around him.
>
> —JOHN 13:3–5, NIV

Jesus washed the dirty feet of His disciples. It was scandalous. Even Simon Peter tried to stop Him, but Jesus kept on washing—even telling Peter that unless He washed Peter's feet, Peter could not be with Him in God's plan. Can you imagine the shock on their faces? He even washed the feet of Judas, the betrayer! Through all this Jesus was teaching His disciples they had to be servants of humanity, willing to do whatever it takes to transform lives.

When you serve, you find out who is real and who isn't. I challenge you to pray for a servant's heart. God will open doors for you to serve as you never imagined. Do it with a heart that doesn't desire a reward. It is with the servant's heart of humility that God will let you stand tall.

4. Authority—God is the author of it

Jesus not only knew who He was, but He also walked in a supernatural authority. When He walked the earth, demons trembled. He never allowed fear, anger, hurt, or despair to rob Him of His authority. His authority came from His Father: "Then Jesus came to them and said, 'All authority in heaven and on earth has been given to me'" (Matt. 28:18, NIV).

Nothing stopped Jesus in His pursuit of fallen humanity. The Bible says He went around preaching, teaching, and healing. His authority came from not only His divinity but also His humanity. He humbled Himself in such a way that His authority was never misconstrued as pride.

Jesus sought out His Father in prayer when He awoke every morning. He always knew His Father had His back. He declared that His words originated from the Father: "I don't speak on my own

---

Five Truths the Remnant Needs to Know About Serving

1. **Use what you have to serve.** Jesus had a towel, and He used it.

2. **People battling the self will try to stop acts of servanthood.** Simon Peter was in a personal war, and he tried to stop Jesus from washing his feet (John 13:8). We later see Peter still battling the concept of being a servant.

3. **A true servant knows how to pick up a towel.** Peter was a man of war—he was the one who grabbed a sword to defend Jesus. But Jesus had a towel.

4. **A servant cleans up after others.** Jesus knew where these men had walked. They had walked on roads made from animal dung. Their feet were filthy. But a true servant washes off the dirt of where others have been.

5. **Be willing to serve those who will harm you.** Jesus washed the feet of Judas—the man who would betray and sell Him to the religious rulers. Yet Jesus loved him enough to wash his feet.

---

authority. The Father who sent me has commanded me what to say and how to say it" (John 12:49, NLT). He could calm the waves with a whisper, curse a tree with a command, and heal a child controlled by a demon. When His authority was questioned by the Pharisees, He never wavered (Matt. 21:23–27). Even the demons begged Him to leave them alone! And when it came time to go to the cross, He submitted Himself to the authority of the Father. He declared, "Not my will, but yours be done" (Luke 22:42, NIV).

Like Jesus, you and I must realize the authority we hold because of the One who lives in us and flows through us. God has called us to take dominion over the earth (Gen. 1:28). This directive was originally given to man and was robbed of man by Satan in the garden. When man decided he was wiser than God, we lost our authority. When Jesus came and died, He restored dominion for you and me:

> Yet the rescuing gift is not exactly parallel to the death-dealing sin. If one man's sin put crowds of people at the dead-end abyss of separation from God, just think what God's gift poured through one man, Jesus Christ, will do! There's no comparison between that death-dealing sin and this generous, life-giving gift. The verdict on that one sin was the death sentence; the verdict on the many sins that followed was this wonderful life sentence. If death got the upper hand through one man's wrongdoing, can you imagine the breathtaking recovery life makes, sovereign life, in those who grasp with both hands this wildly extravagant life-gift, this grand setting-everything-right, that the one man Jesus Christ provides?
> —Romans 5:15–17

God has placed His Spirit inside of us to produce freedom not only in our lives but also in the lives of others. The remnant must choose to exercise that God-given authority. We can pray for the sick and they shall be healed (James 5:15). We can lead our homes into freedom. We can cast out demons in His name and they must flee (Mark 16:17). When we allow fear and disbelief to take over our lives, we have removed God from the throne of our lives and replaced Him with human concepts. We must realize our authority comes from God (Josh. 24:15).

There is such a freedom that comes with knowing you never walk into a room alone. God is with us in all circumstances. Here is the greatest passage in the Bible for protecting your God-given authority:

> Finally, be strong in the Lord and in his mighty power. Put on the full armor of God so that you can take your stand against the devil's schemes. For our struggle is not against flesh and blood, but against the rulers, against the authorities, against the powers of this dark world and against the spiritual forces of evil in the heavenly realms. Therefore put on the full armor of God, so that when the day of evil comes, you may be able to stand your ground, and after you have done everything, to stand. Stand firm then, with the belt of truth buckled around your waist, with the breastplate of righteousness in place, and with your feet fitted with the readiness that comes from the gospel of peace. In addition to all this, take up the shield of faith, with which you can extinguish all the flaming arrows of the evil one. Take the helmet of salvation and the sword of the Spirit, which is the word of God. And pray in the Spirit on all occasions with all kinds of prayers and requests. With this in mind, be alert and always keep on praying for all the saints.
>
> —EPHESIANS 6:10–18, NIV

I will never forget the battle we faced in China when we adopted our daughter, Abby, and how it became an opportunity to exercise our God-given authority with victory. When we arrived in China, we finally held our daughter in our arms. The process of adoption wasn't complete, so we spent two weeks traveling to several provinces to complete the paper-work required for her to become ours. The first night at the hotel with our new gift from heaven was just magical. We couldn't believe God had trusted us with such a gift. She had several infections in her body, so we went to work helping her get healthy. Karen spent hours nursing her back to health.

During our second night with Abby, she began to experience what are known as "night terrors." Night terrors are described as "a sleep disruption that seems similar to a night-mare, but with a far more dramatic presentation."[2] Abby began to wake up every couple of hours screaming out in fear. Every time she would begin to rest soundly, a terror would hit her body. This went on for several days, and we were simply at our wits' end, not knowing what to do to help her. We were exhausted and frazzled while finishing the adoption process so we could take her home.

After days of no sleep, I had had enough. Late one night, as the rest of the family slept, the Lord spoke to me to turn on some worship music on my laptop. I turned it on quietly so as not to awaken anyone, and I began to pray in the Spirit for my family.

Suddenly I saw a giant demonic spirit standing in the corner of the hotel room, but I had no fear. Instead I experienced what I believe was righteous anger. I pointed at the demonic figure and demanded it leave my daughter alone. I said that she now belonged to me and had my name as hers. As I rebuked the demon and commanded it leave, I watched it go out the window of our hotel room. Since that night my daughter has never experienced another night terror. Her father exercised his God-given authority that comes through Christ on her behalf.

The story doesn't end there. The next day, as we traveled by plane to another province, Karen whispered to me, "I saw it."

"What are you talking about?" I asked.

The remnant hides in the shadows
of intercession only long enough to
embody the burden of restoration.

"I saw the demon in the room," she said, "and I heard you command it to leave. I watched it go out the window and leave."

I was overcome with emotion as I realized that I had an obligation and an authority to protect my family!

I challenge you who are reading this book to take authority over your home. God has anointed you to walk in freedom and power. Stand firm and know that God will back you up. Tell Satan to get away from your house, your family, your marriage, your bodies, your finances, and your dreams. You are a temple and not a shack. God has inhabited you. You have the authority to stop the enemy in his tracks. Take back your dominion. The most dangerous Christian is the Christian who actually understands the weapons God has given us.

Now, I'll ask you one last time: Are you like Him? If so, then you are closer to becoming His remnant. The world doesn't need another cool preacher or another stage showman to be the voice of God. What the world needs most is someone who simply represents the Savior. You are His representative!

Chapter 10

THE OSCAR GOES TO...

Then those who feared the LORD talked
with each other, and the LORD listened and
heard. A scroll of remembrance was written
in his presence concerning those who
feared the LORD and honored his name.

—MALACHI 3:16, NIV

Dear Remnant,
If the world is worshipping you and
you're enjoying it, then somewhere along
the way, Jesus left the room.

JUST GOT 'BIG-TIMED' by him."
Those were the words I heard a pastor friend of mine say
who is leading a powerful youth movement in California. He
was saying it in reference to how a guest speaker had treated
him. The guest speaker came to speak at one of my friend's
youth conferences, and during his time there he made out-
landish demands and acted as if he was a celebrity.

My heart grieved for my friend, but I knew exactly what
he meant when he said he had been "big-timed." I have, over
the years, had to do a gut check on myself as an evangelist
who has traveled over two million miles. It is easy to begin to
believe that you are the greatest voice out there. And in a culture that is celebrity-driven, we all battle with a deep desire
to be seen and heard.

But this is not God's plan for any of us. My friend and mentor, pastor Glen Berteau, who at one time worked at the largest evangelistic ministry of the day and watched the moral failure of its leader, once said to me, "God did not call us to drink the oil but rather wear the oil. The oil, if consumed, will make you fat and poison you." I have never forgotten those profound words.

> The remnant says yes to the cross and no to the applause, yes to the altar and no to arrogance, yes to the covenant and no to worldly concepts.

Every generation is looking for a hero, someone who can lead them to the promised land and show them the way to a better life. And the church is not absent in this endeavor. It seems every few years someone rises to the surface and becomes the face of the church to the populace. And this isn't necessarily a good thing.

Throughout history God has raised up great leaders to be voices of a season for either a weary, disenchanted, or hungry church. I love studying the great voices of the past, such as Smith Wigglesworth, Jonathan Edwards, Aimee Simple McPherson, John and Charles Wesley, Charles Finney, D. L. Moody, William Booth, Charles Spurgeon, and others. Each one of these great remnant leaders not only had something to say, but they were also very human. Some lasted a long time and their legacy continues, and others didn't finish the race as a strong voice.

What makes God's Spirit so special is that He inhabits temples made of dirt.

GET OUT OF THE GREEN ROOM

When the Holy Spirit invades a room, He doesn't care about Christian stature and prominence. He doesn't look at name badges but rather heart cries. By the same turn, when you look at the ministry of Jesus, you get a picture of the stark reality of ministry. Jesus was never in the green room, hobnobbing with the most popular preachers of the day. He was always in the streets rescuing people. He had no microphone. Most of the time He was spending time with those who didn't give in an offering, pat Him on the back, or give Him props for His eloquence.

How did Jesus repay His followers? With pierced hands that couldn't hold a microphone. Jesus never walked the red carpet of premieres. In fact, the closest we get to a red-carpet experience in our Christian history is the blood-soaked trails of the martyrs, and the only roped-off areas we see are the places the Christians were hung.

> The remnant are private worshippers
> with a public voice who seek only
> the revelation of God's kingdom
> and not their own empire.

When we try to build our own empires and not the kingdom of God, we have to be willing to take responsibility when those empires crumble to the ground. We are on very dangerous ground when we begin to believe we produce the glory. Listen to what Jeremiah says:

> This is what the LORD says: "Don't let the wise boast in their wisdom, or the powerful boast in their power, or the rich boast in their riches. But those who wish to boast should boast in this alone: that they truly know me and understand that I am the LORD who

demonstrates unfailing love and who brings justice and righteousness to the earth, and that I delight in these things. I, the LORD, have spoken!"

—JEREMIAH 9:23–24, NLT

God will never show up in a church service when He doesn't trust those who are ministering. History tells us that any time man gets bigger than God, he is destined for failure. Scripture tells us the same thing: "First pride, then the crash—the bigger the ego, the harder the fall" (Prov. 16:18). God cannot bless a man or ministry that refuses to bow before the one true God. The apostle Paul, in his letter to the Christians at Philippi, had to confront this issue of celebrity ministers:

> It is true that some preach Christ out of envy and rivalry, but others out of goodwill. The latter do so out of love, knowing that I am put here for the defense of the gospel. The former preach Christ out of selfish ambition, not sincerely, supposing that they can stir up trouble for me while I am in chains. But what does it matter? The important thing is that in every way, whether from false motives or true, Christ is preached. And because of this I rejoice. Yes, and I will continue to rejoice.
>
> —PHILIPPIANS 1:15–18, NIV

We are accountable to the mantle, and I don't want to apologize to the next generation for not preparing the way. I must declare "Enough is enough" when it comes to the Hollywood elite of over-graced, perverse-talking, self-indulgent ministers. We must get back to the cross! The apostle Paul would have probably sat these elitist ministers of today down with the Epicureans at Mars Hill and said, "Your hedonism is choking my message! Now, be quiet and keep worshipping at the altar of the unknown God as we continue to fight the good fight."

I cannot begin to tell you how many times I have heard people say of someone, "They fell!" This is the term we use when someone has morally fallen into sin, and my heart has always broken for the wounded followers who are left behind to clean up the mess after a leader chooses flesh over purity. The tears that flow from faces of the spouses as they stand beside such a leader through the very public humiliation of moral failure can be heart wrenching. I wonder about the children who hear the words, "Daddy or Mommy messed up."

How does this happen? What is the process? When or where does the character flaw begin to win?

THE BEGINNING OF MORAL FAILURE

Most of those I've met who walked through a moral failure started out with a true passion for changing the world for Christ, but somewhere along the way they lost their reasoning. As I always say, "We are all only minutes from a moral failure, but Jesus is only a whisper away from your intervention."

I believe the devil allows some very flawed ministers to continue into great success without impediment because he knows when they fall, it will create a monstrous wave of pain. So he sits back and waits. But we must remember God will not be mocked (Gal. 6:7). Just as He didn't allow David to go undiscovered in his sin (2 Sam. 11–12), He will not allow others to trample His grace without consequences. Just because we are able to garner thousands of followers on social media and take our pictures with the hottest young star of the day does not mean the kiss of God is on our ministries.

Remember the Laodicean church in the Book of Revelation? They thought they had it all together. But Jesus gave them a stern warning in Revelation 3:15–19 (NIV):

> I know your deeds, that you are neither cold nor hot. I wish you were either one or the other! So, because you are lukewarm—neither hot nor cold—I am about to spit you out of my mouth. You say, "I am rich; I have acquired wealth and do not need a thing." But you do

not realize that you are wretched, pitiful, poor, blind and naked. I counsel you to buy from me gold refined in the fire, so you can become rich; and white clothes to wear, so you can cover your shameful nakedness; and salve to put on your eyes, so you can see. Those whom I love I rebuke and discipline. So be earnest and repent.

Please understand that I am not casting stones. Rather, I am attempting to say to you, "Please be careful!" Every time another minister falls prey to the lies of the enemy, the world becomes increasingly numb to our message. As we have already learned, God is calling His church back to mourning and weeping. Mourning always produces a prophetic move of God.

If you study the last hundred years of the church, every couple of decades we see the rise of a new crop of celebrities. As their popularity grows, so does the demand to feed the "monster of ministry." If these celebrity pastors are not careful, the sin of pride or self-indulgence takes over. This is usually driven by greed to maintain their status. Many times the preachers even begin to preach a watered-down version of the gospel that ends up sounding like a self-help seminar.

> The remnant seeks to gain nothing
> but always has everything to give.

In 2013 a reality TV show called *Preachers of L.A.* made its debut. The show focused on the private and public lives of several men who lead lives of excess and luxury all in the name of Christian ministry. What these men are doing is a mockery of the very call of God. For so long Hollywood has used the church and its leaders as fodder for ridicule. The problem is multiplied when so-called ministers partner with Hollywood to back up what so many in the secular world believe about preachers.

I am reminded of a quote by Augustine of Hippo that has

brought much clarity to my life. He said, "It was pride that changed angels into devils; it is humility that makes men as angels."[1] The apostle Paul gave us clear instruction to how we are to represent Christ:

> Remember, there is only one foundation, the one already laid: Jesus Christ. Take particular care in picking out your building materials. Eventually there is going to be an inspection. If you use cheap or inferior materials, you'll be found out. The inspection will be thorough and rigorous. You won't get by with a thing. If your work passes inspection, fine; if it doesn't, your part of the building will be torn out and started over. But you won't be torn out; you'll survive—but just barely.
>
> You realize, don't you, that you are the temple of God, and God himself is present in you? No one will get by with vandalizing God's temple, you can be sure of that. God's temple is sacred—and you, remember, are the temple. Don't fool yourself. Don't think that you can be wise merely by being up-to-date with the times. Be God's fool—that's the path to true wisdom. What the world calls smart, God calls stupid. It's written in Scripture, He exposes the chicanery of the chic.
>
> —1 CORINTHIANS 3:11–19

I truly believe that God blesses His servants, but the *Preachers of L.A.* is the opposite of the remnant spirit. There are many amazing leaders in Los Angeles who are not flaunting their wealth instead of proclaiming Christ. My dear friends Jeremy and Christy Johnson lead a congregation called Fearless Church that is exploding with baby Christians who want a real encounter with God. Their new church is transforming lives! And there is the L.A. Dream Center led by Pastors Matthew and Tommy Barnett. That ministry is rescuing and restoring lives in a supernatural way.

Do we honestly believe that God can turn a blind eye to

the dysfunction and perverted representatives Hollywood has handpicked to be the church's voice? I don't think so. They are living a very dangerous dream. "God cannot be mocked" (Gal. 6:7, NIV).

In our feeble attempts to handle the holy things of God, we must remember who the author of life is and not confuse our message with hedonism and self-gratification. The devil is liar. He will do everything he can to promote half-truths.

It reminds me of what John Michael Talbot told me one day. I asked him how he felt about worship music today. After all, he was one of the founders of modern contemporary Christian worship. He told me, "The problem with worship leaders today is that they no longer worship upward toward God but now worship outward toward the crowd."

I have been guilty of this. Once, while I was speaking at a conference of several thousand teenagers, I had an awakening by the Holy Spirit. The worship band on stage was the top worship band in the nation. I was personally so excited to finally meet them. I listened to their music nearly every day on my iPod when I jogged. This group is very pure-hearted, and they usher in the presence of God like very few I have ever seen.

As they ministered on stage, I watched as the crowd worshipped with great intensity. After they ministered, the other guest speaker at the conference got up to speak. I noticed that the crowd wasn't engaged at all. It was as if a large percentage were not even listening, but rather talking and even walking around. What happened to the crowd that was worshipping so intently with the band?

The remnant is not a pulpiteer or public speaker, but rather a resuscitator of life to those who have lost breath.

I was now dreading speaking the next day to this same crowd. Then the Lord spoke to my heart. He said, "They adore the band because they are rock stars to them. Son, if we are not careful, we will raise a Saul generation who loves worship more than Word because it soothes their demons."

Jesus said in John 4:24, "God is spirit, and his worshipers must worship in spirit and in truth" (NIV). We must go deep in worship and Word. The next day I shared those very words from the stage. I was shocked to see thousands of young people run to the altar under conviction. It wasn't my words that brought the crowd to the altar. It was the Holy Spirit moving on the hearts of the students.

The Holy Spirit doesn't need you or me to be a substitute teacher. He knows what He is doing. We are simply His mouthpiece and a clay vessel that He shines through. God didn't call us to be actors on stage! He called us to be real and walk in holiness. It doesn't say anything in the Bible that we must act like the world to win the world. On the contrary, the Bible warns of the wrath of God if we are not preaching truth. Romans 1:18 warns, "The wrath of God is being revealed from heaven against all the godlessness and wickedness of men who suppress the truth by their wickedness, since what may be known about God is plain to them, because God has made it plain to them" (NIV).

Jennifer LeClaire, a minister, writer, and the news editor for Charisma News, recently wrote this powerful indictment in her newsletter:

> When preachers tour like rock stars, it's no wonder sinners flock to stadiums. Of course, preachers holding stadium-sized events packed out with lost souls is awesome—unless those preachers present a hyped-up, watered-down, seeker-friendly gospel that's giving the assurance of heaven while sending people to hell.
>
> I am convinced that too many people who claim to be Christ-followers are not really saved because

too many false teachers and false prophets are propagating a "different gospel" centered on "another Jesus" (see 2 Cor. 11:3–4). I am convinced that many self-professing saints are going to sit right next to sinners in hell when it's all said and done—thanks, in part, to rock-star preachers presenting a hyped-up, watered-down, seeker-friendly gospel.[2]

Those are heavy and very truthful words, and I believe if we are not careful, we will try to seduce the Holy Spirit by our feeble attempts to "rock-star the crowd."

One of the most humble men I have ever had the privilege of being around is Pastor Larry Stockstill. Pastor Larry is considered one of the leading voices in Christianity today. Yet for many years I have watched him lead with amazing authority and purity of heart. Years ago he invited his son Joel, another leader, and me to join him for a day of mentoring at the campus of Bethany World Prayer Center, where he served as pastor for several decades. During that time he shared with us what was then the unfinished manuscript of *The Remnant: Restoring the Call to Personal Integrity*. This book was the tool God used to teach me the concept of remnant. It is a clarion call for leaders to walk free from the trappings of "success" by calling them back to the kind of transparency and integrity that used to mark the church. It asks a sobering question, When did the simple, pure gospel of the Savior become about "me," "my," and "mine"? It is a question that I too must ask.

LET THEM SEE YOUR SCARS

God uses you and me to bring truth and freedom. But I am amazed at how, when we look upon a stage, we see the shimmering armor of modern-day knights. They never allow us to get close enough to see the scars they secured in battle!

I am so glad Jesus let the crowd get close to Him. Think about it—if He hadn't, the woman with the issue of blood would never have been able to touch Him and be healed. Blind Bartimaeus never would have been healed. The man with the withered hand never would have gained a perfected limb. The ten lepers would have gone on being lepers. The woman with the alabaster jar never would have anointed His feet with perfume and tears.

> The remnant doesn't need the stage but rather a place to call home to bring a weary guest.

The stage has the ability to make you forget the crowd in front of you. I can speak to this from experience. One day I was praying and weeping before the Lord. On this particular day my prayer closet had become a whiner's den. I was complaining to God about difficulties I had faced over a period of time. It just didn't feel that our ministry was going to another level.

The Lord spoke to me and said, "Pat, when did your ministry become yours? Son, do you remember when you promised Me that your ministry would always belong to Me?"

I said, "Lord, this ministry *is* Yours. Please forgive me!"

He responded and said, "Pat, if they can see you, then they can't see Me. Just be a stagehand and lift the curtain for My glory. Then get out of the way. Allow Me to always shine."

This was one of those "come to Jesus" moments for me. It helped set me and my attitude—not to mention my ministry!—back on the right track. But what if I hadn't found my way into the prayer closet? The results might have been unpleasantly different.

Look what the apostle Paul said concerning how we should act:

> Therefore, my dear friends, as you have always obeyed—
> not only in my presence, but now much more in my
> absence—continue to work out your salvation with

fear and trembling, for it is God who works in you
to will and to act according to his good purpose. Do
everything without complaining or arguing, so that
you may become blameless and pure, children of God
without fault in a crooked and depraved generation, in
which you shine like stars in the universe.
—Philippians 2:12–15, niv

If you want to be a star for God, then you have to shine
with purity and truth. It isn't about whom you know, where
you have ministered, or who endorses your ministry. It is
about leading the sheep—and being shepherds who smell
like sheep. When we get to a place where we no longer like
the sheep, we have lost our way and must be found.

> The remnant does not walk in flattering
> circles but rather in the places where
> the unknown sojourner must be found.

When we rescue the hurting, we are reminded of our original calling. But when our honorariums or love offerings
become an amount we demand in order to keep up our lifestyle, we lose our focus on the "least of these."

The people Jesus considered the celebrities of His day were
the children. When His handlers, the disciples, tried to keep
them from Him, He got angry. He went so far as to declare
to the disciples, "The kingdom of heaven belongs to such as
these" (Matt. 19:14, niv).

Get Back to the Cave

It is in the cave that God can reshape our thinking and
remold our hearts. There have been times where I have
prayed that God would put me in His cave, because these are

the times that He speaks the loudest and draws me back to my priorities.

I call it a cave because God used the cave many times to rescue and restore His leaders. He protected His people in caves in 1 Samuel 13:6: "When the men of Israel saw that their situation was critical and that their army was hard pressed, they hid in caves and thickets, among the rocks, and in pits and cisterns" (NIV). It was in the cave experience that David began the process of building his army (1 Sam. 22:1). This is where Moses was hidden when God's glory passed by and gave him the revelation to write the first five books of the Bible (Exod. 33:22). It is in the cave that Elijah had God's glory pass by in 1 Kings 19:11. This is where Elijah discerned that God was not in the wind, the earthquake, or the fire, but in the whisper.

We too must get back to the cave. It is in the cave God speaks to His warriors.

My brother, Scott Schatzline, wrote an amazing book called *Hubs*. The book speaks of the importance of being in seasons of transition between each place God takes us. This book deeply touched me, because it is in those "hubs," or "caves," that God has transformed me, just as I shared in the example above about what happened when I went into my prayer closet.

> The remnant will not be swayed by the wind of compromise, will not stare into the eyes of revenge, and will not seek the approval of the populace.

My heart is that you will not end up a casualty of self but a victor of the kingdom of God. Guard the foundation God is putting under you. Learn the power of serving and being teachable. Make yourself accountable, and handle criticism as a guardian of the soul.

Your potential is great, but your flesh will always try to drink the oil instead of wear it. Go back to Genesis and rediscover what caused man to fall. It was the simple promise that they could know more than God.

The cry of the lost must be louder in our ears than the cheer of the crowd. We will never win the world to Christ when we're lost in the celebration of ourselves. The moment we realize we are remnant, we begin rising past our circumstances and personal desires. Your purpose then becomes other people's freedom.

When the populace demands that Christians act like the world and live like the world, God causes a remnant to rise up and stand for truth and not bow to culture. Remember the guideline put in place by the apostle Paul when he wrote, "Follow my example, as I follow the example of Christ" (1 Cor. 11:1, NIV).

TAKE CARE HOW YOU DRESS YOURSELF

Do you remember that story about the emperor's new clothes? It's about an emperor who wanted to wear the fanciest clothes money could buy. This desire so consumed him that he never focused on his kingdom. He never worried about protecting his people or paid attention to the advancement of intruders.

One day two fakes came to the gates of the city. They declared they made the best clothes an emperor could wear. They were brought before the emperor, where they shared with him that they could make the most beautiful clothes that had ever been made—for a large sum of money and gold. Then they said the secret to their clothes was two things: (1) only the smartest people would be able to see the clothes, and (2) only those who rightfully belonged in their position would be able to see the clothes.

The emperor begged these two men to make him their clothes. And so they acted is if they were. They asked for more and more money as they worked in secret at their imaginary loom. When the king sent advisors to see the clothes—which were actually invisible—the advisors bragged about them and declared, "Aren't they beautiful?" Of course, the advisors couldn't see the clothes because the clothes did not, in fact, exist, but in fear of not being seen as smart or not being able to keep their positions, they told the emperor the clothes were just amazing.

> The remnant includes the apostle with worn-out garments, the smiling prophet, the transparent pastor, the weeping missionary, the teacher with tools in hand, and the servant evangelist.

Finally the emperor was invited to see the clothes. He too could see nothing. But as the two fakes acted as if they were putting the clothes on him—with everyone seeing how naked he was—the emperor dared not utter he couldn't see them. Doing so would mean admitting he wasn't smart and didn't belong in his position.

Naked, the emperor went before the people. The people knew the rules about the clothes, and so they cheered as if they could see them. But as the naked emperor led a parade for his new clothes, a little boy cried out, "But he is naked!"

The emperor had bought into the lie that he was above the ability to be transparent—therefore, he ended up naked. There is so much we can learn from this metaphorical story. For instance, is it possible...

- To be so self-indulgent that you refuse to realize when you're naked?

- To have people around you who are so worried about position that they won't be honest with you?
- To be so wrapped up in image that you ignore the kingdom?
- To be so overwhelmed with self that your fear of failure never allows those around you to see the real you?
- To be so self-absorbed that the enemy can deceive you into purchasing an identity that leaves you nude?
- That in the midst of your parade people could be singing your praises while children see the real you?

Every leader fears overexposure to the reality of how they're really dressed. Truthfully, I have prayed more than once, "Please, Lord, don't let them see the real me. The real me is tired, weary, and at times very carnal. Lord, please cover my nakedness. Clothe me, God, with righteousness!"

So often we get dressed for the world and forget to be clothed to meet the Savior. It is so easy to get drunk off our own vineyards that we end up like Noah, naked in front of our family (Gen. 9:20–21). Nakedness is always a metaphor for one's spiritual state, but God is looking to clothe us with His blessings: "Real help comes from GOD. Your blessing clothes your people!" (Ps. 3:8).

We aren't meant to be adorned with self. Rather, God gives clear instructions as to how we ought to dress: "Then adorn yourself with glory and splendor, and clothe yourself in honor and majesty" (Job 40:10, NIV). We must be dressed as priests again!

God has prepared a new outfit for us that represents Him: "Always be clothed in white, and always anoint your head with oil" (Eccles. 9:8, NIV). The white represents the call to purity, innocence, and cleanliness. In other words, we are called to be clothed differently than the world. It was when Adam and Eve sinned that God found it important to cover their nakedness. Genesis 3:21 states, "The LORD God made garments of skin for Adam and his wife and clothed them" (NIV). It was the Laodicean church that needed to be dressed: "Here's what I want you to do: Buy your gold from me, gold that's been through the refiner's fire. Then you'll be rich. Buy your clothes from me, clothes designed in Heaven. You've gone around half-naked long enough. And buy medicine for your eyes from me so you can see, really see" (Rev. 3:18).

God created us in the secret place. There we were naked before Him. Leaders who do not visit the secret place forget when it is important to wear clothes. God is calling His leaders back to transparency and purity. We must not ignore those around us who will tell us when we are naked.

It is time to get dressed. Time is running out! Revelation 16:15 states, "Keep watch! I come unannounced, like a thief. You're blessed if, awake and dressed, you're ready for me. Too bad if you're found running through the streets, naked and ashamed."

We may take to Twitter to proclaim how great we are, and we may Facebook our newest message. We may promote our ideas, and we may declare we are a voice to a generation—yet we rarely get honest about our spiritual state. Joel 2:13–14 says:

> Change your life, not just your clothes. Come back to GOD, your God. And here's why: God is kind and merciful. He takes a deep breath, puts up with a lot, this most patient God, extravagant in love, always ready to cancel catastrophe. Who knows? Maybe he'll do it now, maybe he'll turn around and show pity. Maybe, when all's said and done, there'll be blessings full and robust for your GOD!

Our approach must change!

There is a stirring in my heart for a cleaning up of the

priesthood. We have created such an image that if we fall, people will just move on to a new celebrity.

The world wants priests who look like them, act like them, and even lead like them. The world has always cried out for compromise. In John 18:40 the people cried out, "Give us Barabbas!" (NIV). Remember, the people didn't want Jesus; they wanted a murderer. "No, not Him!" they cried. "Give us Barabbas! Give us somebody who looks like us. He is much easier to look at than Jesus. Jesus reminds us what we should be, while Barabbas gives us the excuse to say, 'I'm not that bad.'"

But we must be different.

THREE GUIDELINES FOR STAYING ON TRACK

Given the pressures of the world and the reality of our flesh, it's not easy to stay on track—and yet it is essential to the cause of Christ. Here are three reminders that can help us stay in the place we're meant to be along the way.

1. Remember who rescued you.

Always remember God is your rescuer. Man did not rescue you. Position and applause will not keep you. God was the One who reached into your dark cell and unlocked the prison doors—and God will always be there to rescue you.

> Some of you were locked in a dark cell, cruelly confined behind bars, punished for defying God's Word, for turning your back on the High God's counsel—a hard sentence, and your hearts so heavy, and not a soul in sight to help. Then you called out to God in your desperate condition; he got you out in the nick of time. He led you out of your dark, dark cell, broke open the jail and led you out. So thank God for his marvelous love, for his miracle mercy to the children he loves; he shattered the heavy jailhouse doors, he snapped the prison bars like matchsticks!
>
> —PSALM 107:10–16

2. Have an attitude of gratitude.

God is using the ones who are broken, torn, and tattered. When He gets them healthy, they don't live their lives in arrogance and pride but rather thankfulness. Thankfulness is a sign you didn't do it on your own!

> Do you see what we've got? An unshakable kingdom! And do you see how thankful we must be? Not only thankful, but brimming with worship, deeply reverent before God. For God is not an indifferent bystander. He's actively cleaning house, torching all that needs to burn, and he won't quit until it's all cleansed. God himself is Fire!
>
> —HEBREWS 12:28–29

3. Remember where you came from.

You didn't just "arrive." People helped you. People believed in you. People sacrificed for you. You're not an overnight success but rather a God project!

> When I was desperate, I called out, and GOD got me out of a tight spot.
>
> —PSALM 34:6

Glance over your shoulder at your past so you recognize it in those you meet in your future. In other words, when you live your call with one finger on the pulse of God and the other on the pulse of humanity, an aligning takes place with both God and man's heart.

God has a greater reward for you than the world could ever offer. His reward comes on the day of accountability, where we will receive crowns we will be allowed to throw at His feet. Those crowns will be adorned with the jewels of souls we helped lead to the cross. That, my friend, is what I call the true definition of winning, for it is far more important to be remnant than relevant!

Chapter 11

THE EMOTION COMMOTION

There will be a highway for the remnant of his
people that is left from Assyria, as there was
for Israel when they came up from Egypt.
—ISAIAH 11:16, NIV

Dear Remnant,
Now is not the time to end up as a
broken-down vehicle of hope on the high-
way of holiness. Guard your emotions
by guarding your heart. We must be the
steady ones!

FOR MANY YEARS there's been a trend along the highways
of America to place white crosses as memorials to those
who lost their lives at a certain point on the road in an accident. I was astonished to see the same trend along the roads of
other foreign nations. These makeshift memorials have been
built as a reminder of the loss of a friend or relative in that
particular location.

One night, as I was driving along I-65 South outside
Nashville, Tennessee, I noticed one of these large memorials
on the side of the road. I felt the Holy Spirit prompting me to
pull over and look at the two large white crosses surrounded
by teddy bears, flowers, and high school paraphernalia. It was
very dark and rainy that night. As I pointed the headlights of
my car toward the memorial, I was overwhelmed with grief

for the families of the two sixteen-year-olds who had lost their lives in a car accident along that part of the highway.

I wondered what it was like for those parents to receive a knock at their door by a state policeman and to hear the words, "There has been an accident." I imagined the grief that must have overwhelmed the families with this horrendous news. These two teenagers had started out on a journey only to have their lives cut short. The agony of lost potential stung my heart as I grieved for these two lives I had never met. I began to pray for the families.

As I slowly edged my car back on the road, God reminded me of the "highway of holiness" mentioned in Isaiah 35:8 (NIV):

> And a highway will be there; it will be called the Way
> of Holiness. The unclean will not journey on it; it will
> be for those who walk on that Way; wicked fools will
> not go about on it.

> The remnant has decided that, at
> all costs, they will not quit on the
> One who would not quit on them.

It reminded me there are many who have crashed on the "highway of holiness." These are what I call the "Should've Beens"—those who should have been a lot farther on their journey but somehow instead found their journey cut short; they ended up as a memorial on the side of the road. They had potential! They had zeal! They may even have had a great ministry vehicle. But somewhere along the way they crashed. Maybe it was a head-on collision with something bigger than themselves, or maybe they simply lost control of the vehicle. Now they are just a memory of what could have been. They are forever a question mark of "What if?"

One of the saddest moments in life is hearing about

someone's influence to change the world being cut short as they become a needless casualty. King Solomon had a lot to say about such lost potential in the Book of Proverbs. Here's one such instance: "The highway of the upright avoids evil; he who guards his ways guards his life" (Prov. 16:17, NIV).

We must make the "highways" safer for people to travel. How do we do that? By establishing first that we will adhere to the laws established for God's "highway of holiness."

THE FRAILTY OF EMOTIONS

The greatest cause of accidents on this highway is not guarding our emotions. Emotions have the power to stop our forward motion and cause us to spin out of control. My dad used to always say to me, "When you lose control of your emotions, there is another force at work driving your emotions."

> Keep vigilant watch over your heart; that's where life starts. Don't talk out of both sides of your mouth; avoid careless banter, white lies, and gossip. Keep your eyes straight ahead; ignore all sideshow distractions. Watch your step, and the road will stretch out smooth before you. Look neither right nor left; leave evil in the dust.
> —PROVERBS 4:23–27

If you are truly called to be God's remnant, I guarantee you'll have to fight on the battlefield. The enemy would love to kill you through emotions. Your emotions have the ability to make or break you. We know that Romans 11:29 says that the gifts and callings of God are irrevocable, so we must make up our minds early in the call of God to never quit. You do not possess the right to do so.

WHEN LEADERS HURT

One of the greatest attributes that a minister must possess at all times is an ability to truly feel the pain of the hurting, distraught, and weary—but what about when we, as leaders, are the ones who are hurting? Who is there to walk with us? Many times in a ministry leadership role the safest thing to do is to just push forward. This is also the most dangerous thing you could possibly do. I once heard it said, "Hurting people hurt people!" I used to say when I pastored, "I wish someone would call and give me the same advice and counsel I give to people when they are hurting." Alas, most of the time that simply wasn't a reality.

The fact of the matter is that most in ministry deal with great hurts, and they have had to learn to bear their own burden. Every great leader faces seasons where hope seems so far away. The writer of Proverbs said it best: "Hope deferred makes the heart sick, but a longing fulfilled is a tree of life" (Prov. 13:12, NIV).

Here's the truth as I've experienced it: most leaders are, at any given time, fifteen minutes away from wanting to quit. Whether this desire to quit is caused from criticism, small crowds, or just plain weariness, it is an epidemic in ministry today. I have learned, though, that God never uses a man or woman He can easily get rid of. My goal is simply to tell you to hold on. God is only as far away as your knees are to the ground. He is standing over you, around you, and beside you. Jesus faced every emotion you possibly could face according to Hebrews 4:15.

We must stop the epidemic of resignations and moral failure in the ministry. God has called you to finish strong! As my wife, Karen, shared with me one day, "'You're better than your critics say and more human than your fans suggest.'[1] Don't be ruled by the critics or the accolades. It is time we rise up and do what we are called to do regardless of the critics or the praise."

Paul warned us to get our act together if we are going to lead:

I have a special word of caution for you who are sure that you have it all together yourselves and, because you know God's revealed Word inside and out, feel qualified to guide others through their blind alleys and dark nights and confused emotions to God.

—ROMANS 2:19–20

The enemy's number one goal is to not make you sin or fall away, but simply to bring you to a place of ineffectiveness. The enemy knows your influence will diminish, and you will essentially be removed from the battle. I say, "Enough is enough." God didn't call each of us to live in the darkness of pain but rather to be an example of true freedom and authority.

In a previous chapter I shared how I personally struggled with what I call a "failure spirit" for years. This is a crippling emotion that usually comes from deep insecurity. It is a spirit that makes a leader feel as if he or she simply isn't good enough to do the work of the Lord.

In the midst of this struggle I heard a profound message from Jeanne Mayo, who has been a spiritual mom in my life over the years. The title of the message was "God of the Dark Times," and it was a message that helped guide me on a journey to freedom. The scripture used as the premise for her message is still one of my favorite verses: "Who among you fears the LORD and obeys the word of his servant? Let him who walks in the dark, who has no light, trust in the name of the LORD and rely on his God" (Isa. 50:10, NIV).

I learned from this message that the end of ourselves is usually the beginning of God. Jeanne explained that regardless of how dark things seem, God is still there. No matter what, God always has His eyes on each of us. When you realize God is always there, you will be able to move past feeling alone.

Unfortunately the desire to quit on God's call is prevalent among God's chosen leaders today. Check out these statistics:[2]

- Each month fifteen hundred pastors quit because of moral failure, spiritual burnout, or contention in their churches.

- The majority of pastors (70 percent) do not have a close friend, confidant, or mentor.

- A little over half of pastors' wives (56 percent) state they have no close personal friends.

- Half of the marriages of pastors will end in divorce.

- Many pastors (70 percent) constantly fight depression.

These statistics are startling. But it is said that all great leaders have great highs and great lows—and the enemy wants to keep you in the darkness. If the enemy can sedate you long enough to keep you from awakening to his attack, then he wins. God has ordained your days, but life exposes you to insecurity, fear, and hurts.

Many leaders I know always seem to be in a battle. Maybe that battle is with people or groups, or maybe it is caused from within, but I must remind you that God has promised in His Word that He can deliver you. You deserve to be a healthy leader. Your family deserves a healthy leader. And believe it or not, God anointed you even with your flaws. Call out to God, and He will direct your "highway"!

Look at the way the psalmist put it:

> I'm feeling terrible—I couldn't feel worse! Get me on my feet again. You promised, remember? When I told my story, you responded; train me well in your deep wisdom. Help me understand these things inside and out so I can ponder your miracle-wonders. My sad life's dilapidated, a falling-down barn; build me up again by your Word. Barricade the road that goes Nowhere; grace me with your clear revelation. I choose

the true road to Somewhere, I post your road signs at every curve and corner. I grasp and cling to whatever you tell me; GOD, don't let me down! I'll run the course you lay out for me if you'll just show me how.

—PSALM 119:25–32

FIVE EMOTIONS DESTROYING LEADERS ON THE "HIGHWAY OF HOLINESS"

If you want to keep from being a casualty on the road of faith, take care to note what's most often taking people out. Mark these five emotions destroying many leaders—and God's response to you if you find yourself hit by any one of them.

1. Depression

This emotion has the ability to cripple even the greatest leader. It can come in like a cloud. It overwhelms leaders to the point that they are crippled. Psalm 88:15 says, "From my youth I have been afflicted and close to death; I have suffered your terrors and am in despair" (NIV).

When we feel as though we do not matter and as if we can't accomplish anything, depression can take root. It is a blinding emotion. The goal is to find your hope again. Colossians 1:13 says, "He has rescued *us* from the dominion of darkness and brought *us* into the kingdom of the Son he loves" (NIV, emphasis added).

I must remind you that darkness never lasts forever. Psalm 139:11–14 states, "If I say, 'Surely the darkness will hide me and the light become night around me,' even the darkness will not be dark to you; the night will shine like the day, for darkness is as light to you. For you created my inmost being; you knit me together in my mother's womb. I praise you because I am fearfully and wonderfully made; your works are wonderful, I know that full well" (NIV).

God knew you before anyone knew you, and He hasn't forgotten you. Just as He knit you together in the womb, He can knit you back together today. What you must understand is that there is a war to stop your future. Hope is your greatest weapon against depression. God can restore your hope. God will restore your hope in the darkest hour:

> No one whose hope is in you will ever be put to shame.... Show me your ways, O LORD, teach me your paths; guide me in your truth and teach me, for you are God my Savior, and my hope is in you all day long.
>
> —PSALM 25:3–5, NIV

2. Insecurity

Insecurity has the ability to rob leaders of their God authority. Hurts and injustice can bring strong leaders under the control of this deceiving emotion. It can cause leaders to believe people are out to get them or that they simply do not matter to others.

When insecurity takes over, you become very dangerous to those around you. This is because insecure people will do everything they can to gain prominence in others' eyes and find security.

> When I felt secure, I said, "I will never be shaken."
>
> —PSALM 30:6, NIV

We must remember the One who called us is always able to deliver us. Get your mind back on Him. Let God restore your security. Think on things above:

> Since, then, you have been raised with Christ, set your hearts on things above, where Christ is seated at the right hand of God. Set your minds on things above, not on earthly things. For you died, and your life is now hidden with Christ in God. When Christ, who is your life, appears, then you also will appear with him in glory.
>
> —COLOSSIANS 3:1–4, NIV

The mind of sinful man is death, but the mind controlled by the Spirit is life and peace.

—ROMANS 8:6, NIV

Your mind must be brought under control just as much as your flesh. When your mind is allowed to run rampant, it will lead you to a destination of pain and destruction. When you allow insecurity to take over your life, you are entertaining a spirit of pride that will bring forth a downfall. Instead, you must be secure in Christ, and the rest takes care of itself.

When you are insecure, you rob others of the joy experienced in knowing God. Insecurity sucks the life out of those who want to follow you. Sooner or later they will be forced to walk away from you just to protect their own self-identity. Instead, you are meant to realize you are God's very best gift to a lost and dying world. You're meant to find your security in the presence of God:

> I know that you, GOD, are on the side of victims, that you care for the rights of the poor. And I know that the righteous personally thank you, that good people are secure in your presence.
>
> —PSALM 140:12–13

I wrote in great detail in my book *Why Is God So Mad at Me?* about the true freedom that comes from understanding the Father's love for His children. For years I battled overwhelming emotions until I realized God loved me regardless of anything.

My good friend Daniel Chua, who pastors City Church in Singapore, recently told me, "If you simply become secure in your sonship, then the heart of the Father is revealed." This sounds so simple, but it is the cornerstone of our salvation and our security:

> What marvelous love the Father has extended to us! Just look at it—we're called children of God! That's who

we really are. But that's also why the world doesn't recognize us or take us seriously, because it has no idea who he is or what he's up to.

—1 John 3:1

Everything about you becomes secure when you realize your Dad walks beside you.

3. Fear

We all know how controlling fear can be, and I have certainly battled this in ministry. I once had to be delivered from the fear of flying. This was a major issue because I fly nearly every week. I have met other great leaders who suffer from panic attacks.

When a leader lives in fear, he or she loses all joy for life. Fear has the ability to create havoc out of thin air. A preconceived mind-set of disaster or offense can destroy or cripple you. But Jesus gave us a promise in Luke 21:14–15:

> Make up your mind right now not to worry about it. I'll give you the words and wisdom that will reduce all your accusers to stammers and stutters.

God can restore your peace! If you are fearful of losing something, you truly don't possess it. Remember what Paul told his spiritual son, Timothy: "For God has not given us a spirit of fear, but of power and of love and of a sound mind" (2 Tim. 1:7, NKJV).

The root of most sin is fear. What do I mean by this? Fear often leads to anger, and anger leads to perversion. Fear is the first stepping-stone to a path of destruction. Make up your mind to trust God instead:

> Trust GOD from the bottom of your heart; don't try to figure out everything on your own. Listen for GOD's voice in everything you do, everywhere you go; he's the one who will keep you on track. Don't assume that you

know it all. Run to God! Run from evil! Your body will glow with health, your very bones will vibrate with life!

—Proverbs 3:5–9

4. Anger

Now, this is a heavy emotion. Anger has the ability to reduce your influence in a matter of seconds. James 1:19–21 instructs us, "My dear brothers, take note of this: Everyone should be quick to listen, slow to speak and slow to become angry, for man's anger does not bring about the righteous life that God desires. Therefore, get rid of all moral filth and the evil that is so prevalent and humbly accept the word planted in you, which can save you" (NIV).

There are certainly times in your life when you have every right to get angry. I even believe there is a right kind of anger. I am talking about the type of anger that rises up when someone harms a child or when injustice has been done to the hurting. But even with that type of anger, we must be careful: "Go ahead and be angry. You do well to be angry—but don't use your anger as fuel for revenge. And don't stay angry. Don't go to bed angry. Don't give the Devil that kind of foothold in your life" (Eph. 4:26–27).

I have personally dealt with anger for years. I could fly off the handle at any moment. Then I began to realize that when I am angry, I do great harm to those who follow me. I also realized my anger affected my family. My family lived on edge due to my emotions. Thankfully God gave me a wake-up call.

God has called us to be wise. Over and over the Bible states that the person who walks in anger has no wisdom.

> Mockers stir up a city, but wise men turn away anger.
>
> —Proverbs 29:8, NIV

> Slowness to anger makes for deep understanding; a quick-tempered person stockpiles stupidity.
>
> —Proverbs 14:29

Did you get that? When you live a life of anger, you're stock-piling stupidity! Anger causes you to lose perspective. It make you forget that ministry is about people. In truth, your leadership position magnifies your anger—and you are supposed to represent God to people. Problems always get multiplied when you get angry. Anger will make you forget your values and make stupid decisions. "An angry man stirs up dissension, and a hot-tempered one commits many sins" (Prov. 29:22, NIV).

The end result of anger is that you live a life of regrets and apologies. Ask God to help you get free. There is something deep there that has to be dealt with. If you are married, have your spouse walk with you through this emotion. And make up your mind to never lose control by establishing trigger points that sound an alarm in your mind. You can be sure these trigger points will go off when you're tired, weary, or offended. Lastly, remember this rule: every time you get angry, someone else is in control.

Personally, when anger begins to enter my life, I immediately go to prayer. I know that if I can get in the presence of God, I will find freedom and joy. We must make sure the only anger we possess is righteous anger and that we use that anger to heal others.

5. Hurts

I have learned offenses have the power to overthrow your emotions as very few other things do. The feeling of being defrauded or abused will cause any leader to immediately step into a defensive position. But God is our defense! God will always get your back:

> But you, GOD, break out laughing; you treat the god-less nations like jokes. Strong God, I'm watching you do it, I can always count on you. God in dependable love shows up on time, shows me my enemies in ruin.
> —PSALM 59:9–10

God has called you to set the captive free (Isa. 61:1), and that will be impossible if you yourself have been taken captive, which is exactly what happens when you have been hurt.

It is so easy to step into the role of being hurt in ministry. It is so easy to get offended when people speak badly of you or simply do not know the wars you're fighting. Yet God has called you to walk in perfect love, which casts out all fear (1 John 4:18). You have to lay your hurts down in order to heal others' hurts.

Offenses cause you to throw up the fences, but you are not called to shrink back. God has called you to look past offenses and see the motives of man's heart. Learn the wisdom of seeing people's motives, and it helps you understand their actions.

Also, it's never personal when it is spiritual. Ask God to give you discernment. This will allow you to judge correctly.

How do you get healed? You have to go back to where it happened and start over. Ask God to show you the root of rejection. Choose to move forward. Make up your mind this pain will not stop you, but rather you will use it to heal others. If you do not get free, you can so easily fall prey to a life of mechanical ministry.

> The remnant does not walk in fear of man's retribution but rather in fear that man will never know the love a Savior.

These five emotions can destroy you, but with God's help you can get free. You are too important and valuable for these emotions to control you. God has amazing plans and dreams for your life. He has called you to rescue the hurting and lost, but you will never be able to do that if you are the one who is hurting and lost. Rise up and lead! There is a world in need of you. No one can harm or stop your destiny when you walk with God. He has your life in His hands. You don't have to fear man or circumstances.

Even Elijah Hurt

One of my favorite people in the Bible is Elijah. This prophet was a rescuer of the remnant. God used him to protect the anointing in a day when all the prophets were being hunted and murdered by Jezebel.

I love the life of Elijah. Why? Not just because he was powerful in his faith. Not just because he is the only man to ever ride a tornado to heaven, but also because he best represents what a leader feels when they are at the end of themselves. Elijah understood a simple fact in ministry that my friend Pastor Donald Gibson of Mercy Gate Church in Houston, Texas, once told me: "People will always love your anointing, but they will not be able to handle your humanity."

The story of Elijah is significant. He had just had an unbelievable victory. He had called fire down on the prophets of Baal (1 Kings 18:36–40). This day was definitely a "win" for him. If this had happened today, he probably would have sent a newsletter to the whole world with pictures and testimonies about what happened.

How is it, though, that a leader can walk out of his greatest accomplishment and then find himself living in a dark cloud? That's exactly what happened to Elijah—and I'm guessing you know what that's like. Elijah was at the end of his rope and was ready to give up. The Bible says, in 1 Kings 19:1–4, that Elijah got word that Jezebel wants to kill him. So Elijah ran for his life. In fact, he even became suicidal: "'I have had enough, LORD,' he said. 'Take my life; I am no better than my ancestors'" (1 Kings 19:4, NIV).

The Elijah Plan for Emotional Restoration

Elijah eventually got free of his moment of despair. How? First Kings 19 shows us a plan that worked for him—the steps he took that kept him from quitting and giving up. I believe this plan will work for us as well.

1. **Lay down and rest.** "Then he lay down under the tree and fell asleep. All at once an angel touched him and said, 'Get up and eat'" (v. 5, NIV).

2. **Get up and eat.** "He looked around, and there by his head was a cake of bread baked over hot coals, and a jar of water. He ate and drank and then lay down again. The angel of the LORD came back a second time and touched him and said, 'Get up and eat, for the journey is too much for you'" (vv. 6–7, NIV).

3. **Get back on the road.** "So he got up and ate and drank. Strengthened by that food, he traveled forty days and forty nights until he reached Horeb, the mountain of God" (v. 8, NIV).

4. **Find a cave.** "There he went into a cave and spent the night. And the word of the LORD came to him: 'What are you doing here, Elijah?' He replied, 'I have been very zealous for the LORD God Almighty. The Israelites have rejected your covenant, broken down your altars, and put your prophets to death with the sword. I am the only one left, and now they are trying to kill me too'" (vv. 9–10, NIV).

5. **Get in God's presence.** "The LORD said, 'Go out and stand on the mountain in the presence of the LORD, for the LORD is about to pass by.' Then a great and powerful wind tore the mountains apart and shattered the rocks before the LORD, but the LORD was not in the wind. After the wind there was an earthquake, but the LORD was not in the earthquake. After the earthquake came a fire, but the LORD was not in the fire. And after the fire came a gentle whisper. When

Elijah heard it, he pulled his cloak over his face
and went out and stood at the mouth of the
cave. Then a voice said to him, 'What are you
doing here, Elijah?'" (vv. 11–13, NIV).

6. **Talk to God.** "He replied, 'I have been very
zealous for the LORD God Almighty. The
Israelites have rejected your covenant, broken
down your altars, and put your prophets to
death with the sword. I am the only one left, and
now they are trying to kill me too'" (v. 14, NIV).

7. **Use your anointing.** "The LORD said to
him, 'Go back the way you came, and go to
the Desert of Damascus. When you get there,
anoint Hazael king over Aram. Also, anoint
Jehu son of Nimshi king over Israel, and anoint
Elisha son of Shaphat from Abel Meholah to
succeed you as prophet'" (vv. 15–16, NIV). One
of the most powerful things I believe so many
miss in this verse is that Elijah anointed a new
king named Jehu, who would eventually kill
Elijah's archenemy Jezebel in 2 Kings 9:30–33.
What you anoint today in your weariness can
someday be used to redeem your lost emotions.

8. **Find your disciple.** "So Elijah went from
there and found Elisha son of Shaphat. He was
plowing with twelve yoke of oxen, and he himself was driving the twelfth pair. Elijah went
up to him and threw his cloak around him.
Elisha then left his oxen and ran after Elijah.
'Let me kiss my father and mother good-by,'
he said, 'and then I will come with you.' 'Go
back,' Elijah replied. 'What have I done to you?'
So Elisha left him and went back. He took his
yoke of oxen and slaughtered them. He burned
the plowing equipment to cook the meat and

gave it to the people, and they ate. Then he set
out to follow Elijah and became his attendant"
(1 Kings 19:19–21).

Elijah was very close to crashing when God took control
of his vehicle. He had come to a place where he was spinning out of control. Yet God had a plan in place to protect
him. Elijah didn't end up as a cross on the side of the road.
Instead of becoming a memorial of lost dreams, he decided
to make someone else's
dreams come true.

I have often wondered
about the day God used
Elijah to interrupt Elisha's
life. Was it just a normal
morning of the regular
humdrum? Had he prayed
that morning, "Lord, how
long will I have to follow
these oxen?" When you
plow a field, it is done with
diligence and purpose. It is
hard work with the reward
not seen until later in the
season. In 1 Kings 19:19–21

We Serve an "Alone God"

"He alone is my rock and my salvation; he is my fortress, I will never be
shaken" (Ps. 62:2, NIV).

"Find rest, O my soul, in God alone; my
hope comes from him" (Ps. 62:5, NIV).

"Praise be to the LORD God, the God
of Israel, who alone does marvelous
deeds" (Ps. 72:18, NIV).

"For you are great and do marvelous
deeds; you alone are God" (Ps. 86:10, NIV).

we see a young leader who was simply doing his daily chores
and God interrupted him. Along with the interruption of
this nobody, God brought hope once again to the prophet
who was weary. This God encounter would bring hope not
only to the student but also to the teacher.

I believe when Elijah placed his mantle (jacket) on the
back of Elisha, a path was made straight for both of them.
The transfer of the anointing righted the road. Eventually
Elisha would get to watch Elijah take the ride of his life in a
tornado surrounded by the chariots of heaven in 2 Kings 2.

Imagine if Elijah had crashed that day when the world was

closing in on him. Then the Bible would have missing from it one of the coolest stories in the Bible—not to mention the healing of one prophet and the anointing of another God wanted to use.

I challenge you to never become a cross on the side of the road, but rather take up your cross and follow Him. A leader who has control of his or her emotions is letting the world know the remnant has arrived to do the work of God.

SECTION III

THE REMNANT IS MARKED BY HIS PRESENCE

Chapter 12

AWAKEN THE SAMUELS

I will surely gather all of you, O Jacob; I will surely
bring together the remnant of Israel. I will bring
them together like sheep in a pen, like a flock in
its pasture; the place will throng with people.
—MICAH 2:12, NIV

Dear Remnant,
   The moment is upon us—it is time to
awaken those who have fallen asleep.
The alarm clock is going off in the spirit
of man to experience a supernatural life
of power and freedom. Will you answer
the call? God has heard our prayers!

IN JULY 2013 I was ministering at a youth camp in Florida.
One afternoon, while talking on a conference call with two
key prophetic voices in America, I became overwhelmed with
the presence of God. We were discussing an outreach we were
planning to do together for a group of very hurting people.
After hanging up from the call, I was still deeply moved in my
spirit for the love of God to transform a generation.

I decided to go for a quick jog around a lake before heading
to my hotel to prepare for the evening service where I would
be speaking. As I was jogging, I heard the voice of the Lord
say to me, "Son, we must awaken the Samuels! Awaken this
generation to My voice!"

Samuel represents the remnant. He was called by God to

197

be consecrated and set apart. This is what you too are called to be as the remnant.

Set Apart for Something More

Do you know the story of Samuel? It's a truly marvelous one. Samuel's mother, Hannah, made a promise to God that if she was able to have a child, she would give her child to the Lord and consecrate the child to Him (1 Sam. 1:11). So when she conceived and Samuel was born, she gave him to the priest Eli when Samuel was still a very young age. His name in the Hebrew language means "God has heard," because God heard the prayer of his mother Hannah.

> The remnant seeks holy justice with a passion for pursuing the fallen asleep with the knowledge of Him who is awakening the dead.

The Bible says that Samuel "grew up in the presence of the Lord" (1 Sam. 2:21). This was during a time when the house of Eli was out of control. Eli's sons were doing atrocious things that Eli ignored but God could no longer ignore (v. 17). But the Bible says that even in the midst of a house of sin Samuel continued to grow in God (v. 26).

Then one night God interrupted young Samuel's sleep:

> The boy Samuel ministered before the Lord under Eli. In those days the word of the Lord was rare; there were not many visions.
>
> One night Eli, whose eyes were becoming so weak that he could barely see, was lying down in his usual place. The lamp of God had not yet gone out, and Samuel was lying down in the temple of the Lord, where the ark of God was. Then the Lord called Samuel.

Samuel answered, "Here I am." And he ran to Eli and said, "Here I am; you called me."

But Eli said, "I did not call; go back and lie down." So he went and lay down.

Again the LORD called, "Samuel!" And Samuel got up and went to Eli and said, "Here I am; you called me."

"My son," Eli said, "I did not call; go back and lie down."

Now Samuel did not yet know the LORD: The word of the LORD had not yet been revealed to him.

The LORD called Samuel a third time, and Samuel got up and went to Eli and said, "Here I am; you called me." Then Eli realized that the LORD was calling the boy. So Eli told Samuel, "Go and lie down, and if he calls you, say, 'Speak, LORD, for your servant is listening.'" So Samuel went and lay down in his place.

The LORD came and stood there, calling as at the other times, "Samuel! Samuel!" Then Samuel said, "Speak, for your servant is listening." And the LORD said to Samuel: "See, I am about to do something in Israel that will make the ears of everyone who hears of it tingle."

—1 SAMUEL 3:1–11, NIV

Samuel lived in a place where the heavens were quiet and deception lived in the next room. But God protected him, and he stayed pure.

We too live in a time when households are out of control and the enemy is destroying families. Yet God can still raise up a remnant in the worst house. God can help us remain faithful to walk in our integrity.

> The remnant chooses to leave
> a life of compromise for the
> spirit of consecration.

A Call to Wake Up

On that first night when Samuel heard God's voice, God called to him three times. It was the first of many times Samuel would experience the voice of God, and his life would never be the same. His purpose had been birthed. His life suddenly changed.

God is a God of "suddenly." Proverbs 13:12 says, "Unrelenting disappointment leaves you heartsick, but a sudden good break can turn life around." He can suddenly interrupt your life with His voice, just as He did with Samuel and just as He did with me. I never felt like God could use me until one day He interrupted my life. It was 1989, and I was attending college at Southeastern University in Lakeland, Florida. I decided to spend the night in prayer at the prayer chapel. I prayed all night, seeking God about my calling. I knew I was called to do something, but I wasn't sure what. After praying all night, I still hadn't received a word from God.

Later that day I went into the chapel, and the worship team was singing a song that cried out for God to send them to the nations! I began to weep as they sang this song. Then a great missionary named Dr. Mark Buntain walked to the platform to speak. I was standing in the back of the chapel against the wall, and Dr. Buntain suddenly pointed to the back of the chapel right at me. He said, "Young man, come here!" I was shocked! Was he talking to me? He said again, "Young man, come here."

Now everyone was looking at me. I was known around campus as being a crazy jokester. I began to walk toward the front of the chapel. Dr. Buntain walked down to meet me and grabbed me by the collar. I was scared to death. This great missionary was the head of Mission of Mercy in Calcutta, India. He looked me in the eyes and said, "God has called you to the nations! You must prepare yourself for a life of adventure for God!" I said, "Yes, sir," as tears flowed down my face. God had answered my prayer.

It is time to wake up! God has a word for you to declare. No more slumber! No more living your life in a daze! I have learned no one ever prophesies over the quiet days, but it is in the quiet days that you must remain faithful. If you remain faithful to your call, regardless of the monotony, the day will come when God will speak. Be sure to remain vigilant, just as Romans 13:11–14 admonishes:

> But make sure that you don't get so absorbed and exhausted in taking care of all your day-by-day obligations that you lose track of the time and doze off, oblivious to God. The night is about over, dawn is about to break. Be up and awake to what God is doing! God is putting the finishing touches on the salvation work he began when we first believed. We can't afford to waste a minute, must not squander these precious daylight hours in frivolity and indulgence, in sleeping around and dissipation, in bickering and grabbing everything in sight. Get out of bed and get dressed! Don't loiter and linger, waiting until the very last minute. Dress yourselves in Christ, and be up and about!

The remnant declares grace with justice, power with meekness, and joy with accountability.

No matter what you have been through, God can use you. He has called you to be set apart for His purpose. God is jealous for you and expects you to step up and lead. Your voice is needed to transform the world with a message from the throne of God. Like Samuel, you must accept the mantle God has for you. Will you accept it?

No Excuses Allowed

The remnant can no longer blame their upbringing. God is removing your excuses by transforming your past into a testimony. God turns your pain into power! He has called you "according to his purpose" (Rom. 8:28, NIV).

Samuel wasn't bitter about where he had grown up, because he knew whom he had grown in. He didn't hate his mother and father for leaving him at the house of God, but he chose to go to sleep every night with God as his nightlight. He was hidden from the world until it was time for God to use him.

I have learned that the greater the anointing, the greater the isolation. Samuel would go from being the last judge to the first prophet in Israel's history. He would be known as the prophet who restored the altars of God in a time when the "word of the Lord was rare; there were not many visions" (1 Sam. 3:1, NIV). He would be used by God to anoint kings and share prophetic words that protected and rebuked the nation of Israel.

> The remnant knows the gifts of the Spirit are not for the evangelical, charismatic, and Pentecostal talent show but rather weapons of a dying leader who has chosen spirit over flesh and freedom over slavery.

Samuel was the remnant of his day. He would travel the land declaring the truth. There was a time when he was even forced by God to tell King Saul that God had removed His blessing off of the life of the king (1 Sam. 15:23). Samuel didn't rejoice that he had to declare judgment on the house of Saul; he wept instead. But Samuel would then go and anoint a new king named David.

I love the life of Samuel because he never compromised his

anointing. He stayed true to his calling and guarded his integrity. In the same way, we must never mistreat the anointing God has placed on us. He has called us to stand firm. He has called us to walk in integrity. God is awakening the Samuels to His voice. He will anoint the remnant to bring life.

Seven Guidelines for Protecting Your Integrity

Perhaps more than anything Samuel is an example to us of integrity. And not just any kind of integrity—the kind that's lived out when everyone else is doing everything else. How can you walk in similar integrity? Follow these seven guidelines, and you'll be safely on your way.

1. Be honest

Do not pad your résumé or reputation with false or inflated accomplishments. The Bible says God hates a proud look and lying tongue (Prov. 6:17). Be a truth-teller in every area of your life, both in the big things and the little things.

2. Guard your dealings with the opposite sex

If you are married, covenant with the Lord and your mate never to be alone with anyone of the opposite sex. Men, be known as a "one woman kind of man." (See 1 Timothy 3:2; Ephesians 5:33.) Ladies, be known as a "one man kind of woman." If you are single, be careful in your conduct with the opposite sex. Treat them with the respect due a sister or brother in Christ. Avoid those private places where your hormones can override your will and you make a bad decision that can change your life forever.

3. Be careful with money

Be a giver and not a taker. Be honest on your taxes. Pay your bills. Furthermore, realize people who love you will want to be a blessing to you. Develop an attitude of gratitude, but never one of entitlement. Ministers do not deserve, nor should they expect, special treatment. The Lord Jesus will properly reward them when they stand before Him (1 Pet. 5:1–4).

4. Protect your family life

First Timothy 3:4 says leaders must rule their own house well and have children who are in submission with all reverence. Titus 1:6 adds that they must be faithful, "not open to the charge of being wild and disobedient" (NIV). One's family life is often an accurate reflection of his spiritual life. Godly men and women will rear godly children who love Christ and obey the Bible. Few areas of investment will yield greater reward.

5. Maintain solid theological competency

Moral and ethical sins often grow out of a defective biblical and theological life. Failing to cultivate a healthy understanding of theological truth—such as the sovereignty and holiness of God, the sinfulness and depravity of man, the process of sanctification, the necessity of biblical wisdom, and the centrality of Christ and the crucified life—you begin to think and then live in a manner that is foreign to the clear teachings of Scripture. Nothing will be more valuable in avoiding this danger than a steady diet of biblical exposition, whereby you are continually exposed to the totality of God's revealed truth. What you believe will determine how you live. Belief and behavior always go together.

6. Be wise in your model of ministry

You are not called to be a CEO or drill sergeant. You are not called to be a rancher or dictator. You are certainly not called to be a spiritual superstar or celebrity. God calls you to be a shepherd of His sheep.

7. Use your gifting properly

A word of caution is in order at this point. The greater your natural gifts and abilities, the more susceptible you are to entrapment by the seducing sirens of the world. Men and women with charismatic personalities and a commanding presence can operate too easily in the power of the flesh and not the Spirit. They can be deceived into believing their own press and the accolades showered on them by adoring followers. If they are not careful, they can begin to believe they have the right to operate by a different standard. This is the way of foolishness. This is the way that leads to the damage—and potential destruction—of a ministry.

Remnant, if you will do these things, you better get ready for late-night and early-morning God interruptions. Are you ready?

Chapter 13

THE REMNANT THAT GOES HIGHER

Once more a remnant of the house of Judah
will take root below and bear fruit above. For
out of Jerusalem will come a remnant, and out
of Mount Zion a band of survivors. The zeal
of the LORD Almighty will accomplish this.
—2 KINGS 19:30–31, NIV

Dear Remnant,
You are now crossing the point of no
return. Your adventure is about to begin.
Will you climb higher in order to plant
roots below and bear fruit above? You
will not be the first, and you will not be
the last.

I HAVE SEEN GOD move mightily in crowds of thousands, but I must remind you that the true remnant usually consists of a small group who is willing to step up and be used by God. Remember the definition of *remnant* we established at the outset? It means "what is left over, usually a small part, a fragment or scrap, unsold or unused piece of cloth, as at the end of a bolt."

While great crowds can make unbelievable noise and excitement, it is the small gathering of the hungry that has started the greatest moves of God. Will you choose to be part of such a group? I challenge you to gather your friends and cry out to God. Start a remnant that will stand firm. The numbers will grow as you grow in God's strength.

> The remnant always clashes with religion because they know, throughout history, religion has always tried to be the noose around the neck of a Holy Spirit movement.

In fact, I call on you to lead a Holy Spirit revolution for God. It may start as a prayer group, a worship team, or even a breakfast club that is willing to go after God together. But even as I encourage you to do this, I must warn you that the religious class will not understand your passion for God—and that's because they have not had a fresh encounter with God.

Regardless of the response of other people, the remnant must hear—and listen to—the wind of God blowing.

BIRTH OF A REMNANT

The New Testament church was birthed in the Upper Room just fifty-three days after Jesus died on the cross for you and me (John 19:30). It was there that victory over sin was won by the Savior. It was time for a new remnant to rise—and it did!

It is now our turn. Jesus said we would do greater works than He did (John 14:12). How would this happen? Who would help us? Jesus promised He would not leave us as orphans but would give us the Holy Spirit (v. 18).

With that being said, I want to close this book by noticing the remnant that chose to go higher. We know that after Jesus resurrected, He showed up in the Upper Room. He breathed upon the disciples, and they received the Holy Spirit (John 20:21–22). For the next forty days He taught and prepared them for what was to come. Then He made them a promise:

"I am going to send you what my Father has promised; but stay in the city until you have been clothed with power from on high" (Luke 24:49, NIV).

I am always amazed at Jesus's first and last miracles. For His first miracle He turned water into wine at the wedding feast (John 2:9). For His last miracle He poured joy into empty vessels in the Upper Room. I believe these two miracles coincide. And as Jesus prepared to leave the earth and ascend to heaven, He gave a promise that another outpouring was coming. In Acts 1:8 He said, "But you will receive power when the Holy Spirit comes on you; and you will be my witnesses in Jerusalem, and in all Judea and Samaria, and to the ends of the earth" (NIV).

We know, according to the apostle Paul, that more than 500 people heard the command to go the Upper Room (1 Cor. 15:6). Why did only 120 show up? Because those 120 decided they needed more. Those 120 found the cross of grace but knew they also needed the room of fire!

CLIMBING A BIT HIGHER

As those 120 disciples climbed the stairs to the Upper Room, they were desperate for more of God. They had chosen to leave the crowd behind. For ten days they waited on the promise headed their way. They would soon rise up as the tribe of Judah. A remnant that had taken root below now would experience the fruit above!

Here comes the "suddenly" again—this time in wind and the fire. Acts 2:1–4 (NIV) tells us:

> When the day of Pentecost came, they were all together in one place. Suddenly a sound like the blowing of a violent wind came from heaven and filled the whole house where they were sitting. They saw what seemed to be tongues of fire that separated and came to rest on each of them. All of them were filled with the Holy

Spirit and began to speak in other tongues as the Spirit enabled them.

The wind of God poured out on this hungry group of disciples, and it was a remnant that would change the world. Simon Peter preached that day, "The promise is for you and your children and for all who are far off" (Acts 2:39). He was speaking of us! The church was birthed with power and the Spirit that day—and the wind has never stopped blowing. God is still baptizing His remnant in fire.

Three Steps to the Upper Room

1. It was the right time. God chooses timing. Remember—He plans out the *kairos* (appointed) time! These followers were desperate. They waited on the edge of their seats for ten whole days.

2. It was the right attitude. The believers were of one mind and one accord. They checked their religion at the door. Instead, they turned the knob of expectancy, and God met them.

3. It was the right place. God chose a small room—the Upper Room—to birth a movement.

WILL YOU GO UP?

All over the world God is raising up His remnant—whether it is in great youth movements taking place in other countries such as Singapore and Australia or in the churches, ministries, conferences, youth movements, colleges, and schools of ministries located in hundreds of cities across the United States that are leading Holy Spirit movements consisting of remnant believers. I believe these are our best days. Now it is up to you!

Do you have the "remnant spirit"?

1. Have you abandoned the old life for the freedom that comes through Christ?

2. Have you decided that no matter the consequence you will declare God's glory?

3. Have you made up your mind to stay "untangled" from this world?
4. Do you live for encounters with God and lost humanity?
5. Have you made a decision not to be defined by the culture?
6. Will you until your dying breath defend God's Word, the truth, and the innocent?
7. Have you decided that pride has no place in your life and that you are called to weep before the cross?
8. Do you realize that you must always look like Jesus?
9. Have you made up your mind to never think you are bigger than God?
10. Have you decided to run from the celebrity mentality?
11. Have you learned to keep your emotions in check no matter what situation you face?
12. Will you be a voice of passion and purity?
13. Will you step up to the plate and be a leader in this movement?

If you want to be part of the last-day "remnant," submit to God and be accountable to your leader. Only the great understand that being under a covering allows you to never get burned.

God has called you to something real and relevant. Persecution will most definitely come. Stand firm, knowing that God likes you and has anointed you for "such a time as this!" All of the disciples were persecuted. All of those who have stood as God's remnant were persecuted.

First Corinthians 4:11–13 (NIV) says:

To this very hour we go hungry and thirsty, we are in rags, we are brutally treated, we are homeless. We work hard with our own hands. When we are cursed, we bless; when we are persecuted, we endure it; when we are slandered, we answer kindly. Up to this moment we have become the scum of the earth, the refuse of the world.

This is your moment. Time is running out. Are you willing to go up? You have to be willing to climb to another level. You have to say yes to going higher with God. He is calling you to leave behind a mundane life and go on an adventure with Him. Will you accept the call?

> The remnant is afraid of only one thing: that time will not permit all they feel called by God to do.

We must never doubt our calling. We do not possess that right. And I will close this book as I did my last one—with my favorite quote from a man who led a remnant for God nearly 150 years ago:

"Not called!" did you say? "Not heard the call," I think you should say. Put your ear down to the Bible, and hear Him bid you go and pull sinners out of the fire of sin. Put your ear down to the burdened, agonized heart of humanity, and listen to its pitiful wail for help. Go stand by the gates of hell, and hear the damned entreat you to go to their father's house and bid their brothers and sisters and servants and masters not to come there. Then look Christ in the face—whose mercy you have professed to obey—and tell Him whether you will join heart and soul and body and circumstances in the march to publish His mercy to the world.[1]

—WILLIAM BOOTH

This is more than just a spoken word. It is a declaration of truth. We are remnant!

NOTES

Foreword by Sean Smith
1. James Baldwin, "Stranger in the Village," in *Notes of a Native Son* (Boston: Beacon Press, 1955, 2012), 167.

Introduction
1. As quoted in Marshele Carter Waddell and Kelly K. Orr, *Wounded Warrior, Wounded Home* (Grand Rapids, MI: Baker Books, 2013), introduction.

Chapter 1
An Open Letter to the Remnant
1. Billy Graham, "Billy Graham: 'My Heart Aches for America,'" Billy Graham Evangelistic Association, July 24, 2012, http://www.billygraham.org/articlepage.asp?articleid=8813 (accessed November 7, 2013).

2. David Wilkerson, "A Revival of Cleansing," devotional posted at WorldChallenge.org on September 17, 2013, http://sermons.worldchallenge.org/en/node/24319 (accessed November 7, 2013).

Chapter 2
Are You Remnant?
1. David Noel Freedman, Astrid B. Beck, and Allen C. Myers, eds. *Eerdmans Dictionary of the Bible* (Grand Rapids, MI: Wm. B. Eerdmans Publishing Company, 2000), s.v. "remnant."

2. *Holman Bible Dictionary*, StudyLight.org, s.v. "remnant," http://www.studylight.org/dic/hbd/view.cgi?number=T5301 (accessed November 7, 2013).

3. Peter J. Leithart, *1 & 2 Kings*, Brazos Theological Commentary on the Bible (Grand Rapids, MI: Baker Publishing Group, 2006), 255–256.

4. David B. Barrett and Todd M. Johnson, *World Christian Trends AD 30–AD 2200: Interpreting the Annual Christian Megacensus* (Pasadena, CA: William Carey Library, 2001), http://www.gordonconwell.edu/resources/documents/WCT_Martyrs_Extract.pdf (accessed November 7, 2013).

Chapter 3
An Audience of One

1. Wikipedia.org, s.v. "Kairos," http://en.wikipedia.org/wiki/Kairos (accessed November 7, 2013).

2. Sir Francis Drake, quoted in Jeanie Curryer, OC Missionary Prayer Letter, September 1997, as viewed at Bible.org, "A Prayer for the Future," https://bible.org/illustration/prayer-future (accessed November 7, 2013).

Chapter 4
The Tangled and Torn Generation

1. Biblesoft's New Exhaustive Strong's Numbers and Concordance with Expanded Greek-Hebrew Dictionary, PC Study Bible v. 3, copyright © 1994, Biblesoft and International Bible Translators, Inc., s.v. "*damah*, OT:1820."

2. Oswald Chambers, as quoted in Joni Eareckson Tada, "Drawing on Memories," JoniandFriends.org, July 2, 2013, http://www.joniandfriends.org/radio/1-minute/drawing-memories/ (accessed November 8, 2013).

Chapter 5
They Were Wrong!

1. Freedman, Beck, and Myers, eds. *Eerdmans Dictionary of the*, s.v. "Nazareth."

2. Ravi Zacharias, *Recapture the Wonder* (Nashville: Thomas Nelson, 2003), 42–43.

3. Barna Group, "Americans Are Most Likely to Base Truth on Feelings," Barna.org, February 12, 2002, http://www.barna.org/barna-update/article/5-barna-update/67-americans-are-most-likely-to-base-truth-on-feelings (accessed November 8, 2013).

4. Merriam-Webster.com, s.v. "secular humanism," http://www.merriam-webster.com/dictionary/secular%20humanism (accessed November 8, 2013).

5. Merriam-Webster.com, s.v. "hedonism," http://www.merriam-webster.com/dictionary/hedonism (accessed November 8, 2013).

6. David F. Wells, *God in the Wasteland* (Grand Rapids, MI: Eerdmans, 1994), 29.

7. Merriam-Webster.com, s.v. "cognitive dissonance," http://www.merriam-webster.com/dictionary/cognitive%20dissonance (accessed November 8, 2013).

8. Jeff Olson, "Cognitive Dissonance: Why Your User's Brains Hurts," Fuel Your Creativity, December 29, 2011, http://www.fuelyourcreativity.com/cognitive-dissonance-why-your-users-brains-hurt/ (accessed November 8, 2013).

9. Martin Beckford, "Richard Dawkins Interested in Setting Up 'Atheist Free School,'" *The Telegraph,* June 24, 2010, http://www.telegraph.co.uk/news/religion/7849563/Richard-Dawkins-interested-in-setting-up-atheist-free-school.html (accessed November 8, 2013).

10. Barna Group, "Atheists and Agnostics Take Aim at Christians," Barna.org, June 11, 2007, https://www.barna.org/barna-update/article/12-faithspirituality/102-atheists-and-agnostics-take-aim-at-christians#.UmgsXpQ0Clo (accessed November 8, 2013).

11. Walter Russell Mead, "Faith: As Not Seen on TV," *Via Meadia* (blog), *The American Interest,* March 6, 2012, http://blogs.the-american-interest.com/wrm/2012/03/06/faith-as-not-seen-on-tv/ (accessed November 8, 2013).

12. Barna Group, "Americans Concerned About Religious Freedom," Barna.org, January 18, 2013, https://www.barna.org/barna-update/5-barna-update/601-most-americans-are-concerned-about-restrictions-in-religious-freedom#.Umg6PZQ0Clo (accessed November 8, 2013).

13. Ibid.

14. National Abortion Federation, "Teenage Women, Abortion, and the Law," http://www.prochoice.org/about_abortion/facts/teenage_women.html (accessed November 8, 2013).

15. Ibid.

16. It's Your (Sex) Life, "STD Testing FAQs: Why Should I Get Tested?," http://www.itsyoursexlife.com/gyt/std-and-testing-faqs/why-should-i-get-tested/ (accessed November 8, 2013).

17. B. E. Hamilton, J. A. Martin, and S. J. Ventura, "Births: Preliminary Data for 2009," *National Vital Statistics Reports* 59, no. 3 (2010), quoted in Centers for Disease Control and Prevention, "Sexual Risk Behavior: HIV, STD, and Teen Pregnancy Prevention," Adolescent and School Health, http://www.cdc.gov/HealthyYouth/sexualbehaviors/ (accessed November 8, 2013).

18. Michael's House, "Drug Addiction Facts and Statistics," http://www.michaelshouse.com/drug-addiction/the-statistics/ (accessed November 8, 2013).

19. Ibid.

20. Intervention ASAP, "Shocking Addiction Facts and Statistics," http://www.interventionasap.com/FAQ_Intervention_Help.html/ (accessed November 8, 2013).

21. Ibid.

22. Ibid.

23. Ibid.

24. Ibid.

25. Ibid.

26. Nate Silver, "How Opinion on Same-Sex Marriage Is Changing, and What It Means," *Five Thirty-Eight* (blog), *New York Times,* March 26, 2013, http://fivethirtyeight.blogs.nytimes.com/ 2013/03/26/how-opinion-on-same-sex-marriage-is-changing-and -what-it-means/?_r=0 (accessed November 8, 2013).

27. Eyder Peralta, "Court Overturns DOMA, Sidesteps Broad Gay Marriage Ruling," NPR.org, June 26, 2013, http://www.npr.org/ blogs/thetwo-way/2013/06/26/195857796/supreme-court-strikes -down-defense-of-marriage-act (accessed November 8, 2013).

28. FoxNews.com, "California Gov. Brown Signs Transgender-Student Bill," August 13, 2013, http://www.foxnews.com/ politics/2013/08/13/california-gov-brown-signs-transgender-student -bill/ (accessed November 8, 2013).

29. CatholicBible101.com, "Mother Teresa Quotes," http:// www.catholicbible101.com/motherteresaquotes.htm (accessed November 8, 2013).

Chapter 6
The Massacre of the Innocents

1. Jon Hurdle and Trip Gabriel, "Philadelphia Abortion Doctor Guilty of Murder in Late-Term Pregnancies," *New York Times*, May 13, 2013, http://www.nytimes.com/2013/05/14/us/kermit -gosnell-abortion-doctor-found-guilty-of-murder.html (accessed November 12, 2013).

2. Terence P. Jeffrey, "Planned Parenthood Did One Abortion Every 95 Seconds—as Many in One Year as Live in Cincinnati," CNSNews.com, April 8, 2011, http://cnsnews.com/news/article/ planned-parenthood-did-one-abortion-every-95-seconds-many-one -year-live-cincinnati (accessed November 12, 2013).

3. Michael Snyder, "More Than 2000 Children Are Murdered in the United States Every Single Day," The American Dream, December 15, 2012, http://endoftheamericandream.com/archives/more-than -2000-children-are-murdered-in-the-united-states-every-single-day (accessed November 12, 2013).

4. Margaret Sanger, *Women and the New Race* (New York: Truth Publishing Company, 1920), 63. Viewed at Google Books.

5. The White House, "Remarks by the President at the Planned Parenthood Conference," April 26, 2013, http://www.whitehouse.gov/the-press-office/2013/04/26/remarks-president-planned-parenthood-conference (accessed November 12, 2013).

6. Doug Stanglin, "Judge OKs 'Morning-After Pill' for Girls of All Ages," *USA Today*, April 5, 2013, http://www.usatoday.com/story/news/nation/2013/04/05/morning-after-pill-judge-plan-b-girls/2055873/ (accessed November 12, 2013).

7. Freedom4Innocence.org, "Human Trafficking Statistics," http://freedom4innocence.org/human-trafficking-statistics/ (accessed November 12, 2013).

8. International Street Kids, "Statistics on Abandoned Children," http://www.internationalstreetkids.com/statistics.php (accessed November 12, 2013).

9. Child Help, "Child Abuse in America," National Child Abuse Statistics, http://www.childhelp-usa.com/pages/statistics (accessed November 12, 2013).

10. *Human Life Alliance*, "A Chronology of Life in the Womb [Fetal Development]," Christian Life Resources, http://www.christianliferesources.com/article/a-chronology-of-life-in-the-womb-fetal-development-1043 (accessed November 12, 2013).

11. Hurdle and Gabriel, "Philadelphia Abortion Doctor Guilty of Murder in Late-Term Pregnancies."

12. William Robert Johnston, compiler, "Percentage of United States Women Who Have Had Abortions," October 15, 2008, http://www.johnstonsarchive.net/policy/abortion/uslifetimeab.html (accessed November 12, 2013).

13. R. K. Jones, J. E. Darroch, and S. K. Henshaw, "Patterns in the Socioeconomic Characteristics of Women Obtaining Abortions in 2000–2001," *Perspectives on Sexual and Reproductive Health* 34 (2002): 226–235, as referenced in National Abortion Federation, "Women Who Have Abortions," rev. 2003, http://www.prochoice.org/about_abortion/facts/women_who.html (accessed November 12, 2013).

14. Associated Press, "Who's Getting Abortions? Not Who You'd Think," NBCNews.com, January 18, 2008, http://www.nbcnews.com/id/22689931/ns/health-womens_health/t/whos-getting-abortions-not-who-youd-think (accessed November 12, 2013).

15. Lawrence B. Finer, Lori F. Frohwirth, Lindsay A. Dauphinee, Susheela Singh, and Ann M. Moore, "Reasons U.S. Women

Have Abortions: Quantitative and Qualitative Perspectives," *Perspectives on Sexual and Reproductive Health* 37, no. 3 (September 2005), viewed at Guttmacher Institute, http://www.guttmacher.org/pubs/journals/3711005.html (accessed November 12, 2013).

16. The Center for Bio-Ethical Reform, "Abortion Facts," AbortionNO.org, http://www.abortionno.org/abortion-facts/ (accessed November 12, 2013).

Chapter 7
The Simeon Cry

1. Orthodox Church in America, "Holy, Righteous Simeon the God-Receiver," http://oca.org/saints/lives/2013/02/03/100409-holy-righteous-simeon-the-god-receiver (accessed November 13, 2013).

Chapter 8
Weeping Lions and Roaring Lambs

1. Harold Vaughan, "The Great Sin: Some Reasons Why God Hates Pride," http://christlifemin.org/publications/Archive%20Articles/thegreatsin_whygodhatespride.pdf (accessed November 13, 2013).

2. John Piper, "I Do Not Nullify the Grace of God," sermon preached March 6, 1983, http://www.desiringgod.org/resource-library/sermons/i-do-not-nullify-the-grace-of-god (accessed November 13, 2013).

3. Matthew Henry, "Psalms Chapter 56," in *Complete Commentary on the Bible,* http://www.sacred-texts.com/bib/cmt/henry/psa056.htm (accessed November 13, 2013).

4. Leonard Ravenhill, *Heart Breathings in Poetry and Prose* (N.p.: Harvey and Tait, 1995), as quoted in "Excerpts From *Heart Breathings,*" Ravenhill.org, http://www.ravenhill.org/heartb21.htm (accessed November 13, 2013).

5. *Charisma*, "Quotes From David Wilkerson," April 28, 2011, http://charismanow.com/spirit/evangelism-missions/13370-quotes-from-david-wilkerson (accessed November 13, 2013).

6. This quote can be found on numerous websites on the Internet.

7. Dietrich Bonhoeffer, *The Cost of Discipleship* (New York: Touchstone, 1959), 44–45. Viewed at Google Books.

8. Posts and tweets from Bill Johnson's Facebook and Twitter pages.

9. Wikipedia.org, s.v. "Universalism," http://en.wikipedia.org/wiki/Universalism (accessed November 13, 2013).

10. Ravenhill, *Heart Breathings in Poetry and Prose*, as quoted in "Excerpts From *Heart Breathings*."
11. IMDB.com, "*Robin Hood* (2010) Quotes," http://www.imdb.com/title/tt0955308/trivia?tab=qt&ref_=tt_trv_qu (accessed November 13, 2013).

CHAPTER 9
ARE YOU LIKE HIM?

1. GoodReads.com, "Augustine of Hippo," http://www.goodreads.com/quotes/107417-hope-has-two-beautiful-daughters-their-names-are-anger-and (accessed November 13, 2013).
2. Kids Health From Nemours, "What Are Night Terrors?," http://kidshealth.org/parent/medical/sleep/terrors.html (accessed November 13, 2013).

CHAPTER 10
THE OSCAR GOES TO . . .

1. ThinkExist.com, "Saint Augustine Quotes," http://thinkexist.com/quotation/it_was_pride_that_changed_angels_into_devils-it/304337.html (accessed November 15, 2013).
2. Jennifer LeClaire, "When Rock-Star Preachers Spew a False Gospel," Jennifer LeClaire Ministries, May 4, 2013, http://www.jenniferleclaire.org/articles/when-rock-star-preachers-spew-a-false-gospel (accessed November 18, 2013).

CHAPTER 11
THE EMOTION COMMOTION

1. This quote that my wife stated is drawn from Christine Caine's Twitter page.
2. Gateway Collegium, "It Does Not Have to Be This Way," http://gatewaycollegium.com/why-attend-the-collegium/it-does-not-have-to-be-this-way (accessed November 18, 2013).

CHAPTER 13
THE REMNANT THAT GOES HIGHER

1. William Booth, as quoted in Alvin Reid, *Evangelism Handbook: Spiritual, Intentional, Missional* (Nashville: B&H Publishing Group, 2009), 285. Viewed at Google Books.

God is using ordinary people to accomplish extraordinary exploits for His kingdom. In Pat Schatzline's book *I Am Remnant*, you will be taken on a journey that will lead to deeper understanding of truth, spiritual identity, and, most of all, your God-given purpose. This book carries an awakening message that requires a response from all generations.

—CHRIS HODGES
SENIOR PASTOR, CHURCH OF THE HIGHLANDS, BIRMINGHAM, AL
AUTHOR, *FRESH AIR*

Educated people can touch the pulse of a man and tell if his heart is in trouble. Pat can touch the pulse of a generation and tell you if they are remnant. This is mandatory reading for the unsatisfied. Caution: gloves should be worn in handling this book. My longtime friend and minister reveals a blazing mandate for an awakening of an army. This message must be read and adhered to by every believer. Before you declare "I am remnant," read what it means! Your life will be transformed!

—GLEN BERTEAU
PASTOR, THE HOUSE, MODESTO, CA

We're living in a day of great contradiction where "the love of many has grown cold." And yet there is a remnant of people who are crying out for the God of Elijah to once again reveal Himself in the fires of Pentecost and the rains of revival. This separation should be of no surprise as the return of our Lord Jesus Christ draws near. He is separating the chaff and the wheat. He is preparing a bride without spot or blemish. Those of us who feel the compelling of the Spirit to not only have *some* oil but to have *extra* oil are rising up in the power of the Spirit and believing God for nations as our inheritance.

In the midst of this prophetic moment there is a sound that is being released. This sound is a sound of repentance, righteousness, and spiritual reformation. As Paul said, this sound is not something weak or "done in a corner." This sound is a clear call to those of like mind and those who are tired of mundane religion. There is a people who are hearing this sound and responding. The remnant is people of all races, colors, backgrounds, and creeds. They hear the sound to rise and move the gates of hell. They hear the sound to prepare their garments and store up the extra oil. This sound is articulated in great clarity by *I Am Remnant*. Pat Schatzline has once again gone to the mountain of God and returned with fresh manna from heaven. If you think this is your average, run-of-the-mill inspirational book, then buckle your seat belts and get a box of tissues 'cause you will be rocked to the very core of your being!

—JOEL STOCKSTILL
PASTOR AND EVANGELIST, BETHANY WORLD OUTREACH CENTER,
BATON ROUGE, LA

In his new book Pat calls us back to the simplicity of living by the power of the Holy Spirit. This book will impact you so that you can make a lasting impact on this generation.

—BENNY PEREZ
LEAD PASTOR, THE CHURCH AT SOUTH LAS VEGAS
WWW.THECHURCHLV.COM

Pat Schatzline is once again used of the Holy Spirit to pen words of awakening. In this book there is a voice calling sons and daughters into their God-given purpose.

—KAREN WHEATON
EVANGELIST AND FOUNDER, THE RAMP, HAMILTON, AL

Today's world awaits the words of a true prophet who will challenge the church to reach its true destiny. Pat Schatzline has heard this challenge from the heart of God and has placed that passionate plea in his new book, *I Am Remnant*. This author has put the mantle of a true prophet around his shoulders, placed a pen in his hand, and written what God is prophetically saying to the church now. The remnant Pat writes of will be an Isaiah 6 body of believers who will visit the throne room of God and see His glory filling the earth. When they see His glory, their response will be, "Woe is me, for I am undone." In this attitude of humility and repentance the remnant will be touched and cleansed by the coals from God's altar. Then they will hear a conversation among the Godhead saying, "Who will go for us?" Their response, like Isaiah's, will be, "We will go!" This remnant, fresh from the altar of repentance and cleansing, will become a "secret weapon" that will revolutionize the world and demonstrate the kingdom of God. Are you remnant?

—Bishop Tommy Reid
Apostolic leader, The Tabernacle, Orchard Park, NY

I Am Remnant makes the warrior stand up inside wholehearted Christians—just from reading the title! It is more than a book. It is a proclamation, a manifesto, and a declaration. It is a clarion call to a generation that is hungry for a purpose that demands their everything…and a mission that ripples into eternity. In a church world where books abound that console self-centeredness and cheap believism, *I Am Remnant* courageously cuts through the superficial norm. Read at your own risk. Your life will both be challenged and altered.

—Jeanne Mayo
Leadership coach and founder, The Cadre and
YouthLeadersCoach.com

I was in the meeting the first time Pat Schatzline preached the powerful, life-changing message titled "I Am Remnant." Hundreds of people passionately flooded the altars to declare that they would arise from the ashes of obscurity and stand as remnant in the earth. There is a remnant being assembled around the globe, a group of imperfect people who are totally committed to their perfect Savior, a generation who won't quit because Jesus didn't quit on them. The message in this book is not for the weak of heart—it is a clarion call to a generation to emerge as a force and manifest the kingdom of God in a lost culture!

—Shane Warren
Pastor, The Assembly, West Monroe, LA

The question of mankind down through the centuries, even back to the Book of Genesis, is, "Who am I, and what is the meaning of my life?" Included in that are, "Do I have a purpose and destiny? Is my life really significant? Does my past disqualify me from future accomplishments? Should I aspire to do great things for the kingdom of God, and would God really use me?" *I Am Remnant* will answer all these questions, challenge you to aspire to go beyond your perceived limitations, and show you how to live a life of significance and finish life strong and fulfilled. Go for it!

—Dr. Al Brice
Pastor, Covenant Love Church, Fayetteville, NC

The only effective answer to today's momentum of sin is the unleashed power of truth. Pat Schatzline has courageously and compassionately identified the defining focus of today's generation of world-changers. Through *I Am Remnant* believers hear the clear call of God's heart not only to encounter Him but also to receive from God His passion for the broken world.

—Jim Hennesy
Pastor, Trinity Church, Cedar Hill, TX

A remnant isn't merely what remains. A remnant is all that the Lord requires from the whole of what was, continuing His work toward what will be. If you find yourself violated by kingdom complacency or yearning for a demonstrated power of more than great preaching, join Pat Schatzline (and a host of remnant warriors just like you and me) as we find strength in our declaration, "I am remnant!"

—Glenn Walters
Lead pastor, Judah Church
Founder, Shabbach Youth Conferences, Charlotte, NC

I am certain that Pat has hit the nail prophetically on this one. Just a cursory glance through the Scriptures will reveal that it is always through a remnant that God works through, whether it was the seven thousand in Elijah's day, the remnant that returned to rebuild Jerusalem after their release from Babylonian captivity, or the remnant that God has preserved even until now in Israel. May the remnant arise gloriously in this hour, untainted and full of the Spirit of God. This book is a home run.

—Yang Tuck Yoong
Pastor, Cornerstone Church, Singapore

The cry for a genuine, godly, balanced, hands-in-the-dirt remnant is long overdue. As the church vacillates from a hidden-in-the-sanctuary, false-holiness mentality to the current misrepresentation of grace without life transformation, we are in desperate need of a wake-up call! I encourage you to read this book, this message that God has given Pat Schatzline, and allow the Spirit of God to speak deeply to your heart. Are you remnant?

—GEORGE SAWYER
PASTOR, CALVARY CHURCH, DECATUR, AL

Today there is a strong spirit from hell wooing people to bow to the culture of compromise, and God is trying to speak loudly through His prophets to His church. *I Am Remnant* is a message penned by a prophet that declares the difference between relative truth and the absolute truth in the Word of God. We as His people must follow the Holy Spirit in these last days. It's great to hear the voice of the prophet speaking loudly to His church. We must listen now more than ever.

—SCOTT S. SCHATZLINE
LEAD PASTOR, DAYSTAR FAMILY CHURCH, TUSCALOOSA, AL

Pat Schatzline has done it again! *I Am Remnant* is right on target! This book will break the chains of cultural carnality and thus infuse a generation with timeless truth, truth that will sustain an end-time revival of passion, purity, and, most of all, principle. This book will raise up a sold-out remnant speaking truth to a culture seeking truth. I for one am ready. Read the book. Join the movement. I am remnant!

—PAUL OWENS
PASTOR, FRESH START CHURCH, PEORIA, AZ

The book *I Am Remnant* by evangelist Pat Schatzline was first preached at CT Church in Houston, Texas, where I serve as the lead pastor. The message Pat delivered that night was absolutely revolutionary. I knew immediately that God would use that word to touch multiplied thousands of lives. Caution: as you read this book you will find yourself wanting to become a part of the remnant that is rising in these last days.

—DON NORDIN
LEAD PASTOR, CT CHURCH, HOUSTON, TX

A powerful, well-written book about taking a stand for absolute biblical truth in a compromising, relativistic society. Pat Schatzline has written another fantastic book that is a must-read for all parents, teachers, educators, elected officials, pastors, and anyone who cares about the future survival of our country.

—DAVID GARCIA
PASTOR, GRACE WORLD OUTREACH CHURCH, BROOKSVILLE, FL

In his new book, *I Am Remnant*, our good friend Pat Schatzline delves deep into the culture of the remnant and highlights its beliefs and standards and its driving force, which is a deep, intimate relationship with God. In a time when being a part of the remnant is not popular, Pat calls every one of us to live the remnant lifestyle God has called us to live.

—ANDY AND PATTY VALENZUELA
PASTORS, IGNITE MOVEMENT, EL PASO, TX

Some books express ideas and hopes. Some are filled with practical application of great principles. And some books communicate the heart of the author and the passion of a God who is mad about His children. Pat Schatzline has authored such a book. *I Am Remnant* is more than a book. It is the heart cry of a man who has spent the better part of his life raising a remnant for the cause of Christ. If your heart's desire is to be a part of the last-days generation that screams "I am remnant!," read this book. You will not regret it!

—DEN HUSSEY
CAMPUS PASTOR, THE CROSSING PLACE FELLOWSHIP,
MORGAN CITY, LA

Elijah once sat in despair believing that he was the only follower of God. But God revealed that He had seven thousand set aside who had not worshipped a false god. Today God has and continues to set apart men and women who will march to a different beat than the world is offering. These people are remnant. Each one of us has the opportunity to stand up and be counted. Pat Schatzline has heard the call and taken a stand. In Pat's stand he has written a powerfully prophetic book that amplifies the voice of God to our world. I hear the call, and I invite you to join the movement. I am remnant!

—TED MILLER
LEAD PASTOR, CROSSROADS, OKLAHOMA CITY, OK

As I observe today's society and its culture, I realize that there are only a few true Christ followers left behind. Through the book *I Am Remnant* God reminds us that we are called to be the candle holders that contain His presence to shine His light! And while we stand against multitudes, we have nothing to fear because He is with us. We are remnant.

—Eddie Zaldana
Youth director, Spanish Eastern District of the
Assemblies of God

Pat Schatzline is a prophetic voice in our generation. This book speaks to the heart of believers and calls us to the forefront for reaching this world with a message of hope and salvation. I heartily endorse Pat's new book *I Am Remnant!*

—Doug McAllister
Lead pastor, Journey Fellowship Church, Lacombe, LA

Every person has a desire to be part of a winning team. The definition of a winning team in our society today is a moving target, left to the discretion of each person's opinion or philosophy. In his latest book, *I Am Remnant*, Pat Schatzline clearly defines what a winning team looks like. In doing so, he also brings great motivation and credibility to those who dare to stand for truth. The winning team is Team Jesus, and it is made up of those who uphold the standards of God's Word. I proudly recommend this book as a prophetic rallying point for today's remnant.

—Jay Stewart
Founding/lead pastor, The Refuge, Charlotte, NC
JayStewart.tv

I Am Remnant was certainly written for a "time such as this." It is indeed a clarion call to God's twenty-first-century church to return to His first-century vision for its existence. This book is written with honesty and will provoke those who have settled for being "comfortably seated" to arise with a fresh desire to live for God and be a part of His awakened army. What Pat Schatzline has written is a heart cry that has the power to mobilize the church to break the "business as usual" mentality that has infected so much of it. If read, thought about, and applied, this book will create a fresh passion and desire in you to know the King and to advance His kingdom. Well done, Pat.

—Andy Elmes
Lead pastor, Family Church and Synergy Network;
author, God's Blueprint for His Church
www.family-church.org.uk